complete
ROAD BIKE
maintenance

Guy Andrews

Note

Whilst every effort has been made to ensure that the content of this book is as technically accurate and as sound as possible, neither the author nor the publishers can accept responsibility for any injury or loss sustained as a result of the use of this material.

Published by Bloomsbury Publishing Plc

50 Bedford Square
London WC1B 3DP
www.bloomsbury.com

First edition 2013

ISBN (print): 978 1 4081 7093 9
ISBN (epub): 978 1 4081 8647 3
ISBN (epdf): 978 1 4081 8646 6

A CIP catalogue record for this book is available from the British Library.

Cover photograph © Gerard Brown
Inside photographs © Gerard Brown
Designed by Jonathan Briggs

This book is produced using paper that is made from wood grown in managed, sustainable forests. It is natural, renewable and recyclable. The logging and manufacturing processes conform to the environmental regulations of the country of origin.

Typeset in 12pt on 9.5pt Helvetica Neue LT Pro by Jonathan Briggs, London

Printed in China by South China Printing Company, Dongguan Guangdong

10 9 8 7 6 5 4 3 2 1

Acknowledgements

A big thank you to photographer, Gerard Brown; to designer, Jonathan Briggs –
who had a hell of a job on his hands; and to the ever-patient Sarah Cole,
Lisa Thomas and everyone at Bloomsbury.

I'd also like to thank:
Phil, Gill and Roger at Mosquito Bikes for Independent Fabrication and
Pegoretti bikes, many thanks all.
Chris Garrison for Wrench Force tools, Bontrager wheels and Trek bikes.
Jordan Gibbons and everyone at Rouleur magazine.
Rory Hitchens and Dom Mason at Upgrade Bikes for Lezyne and other such
lovely stuff they do.
Shelley Childs at Continental for tyres, tubes and tubulars.
Chris Snook and Albert Steward at Madison for Shimano and Park Tools.
Grant Young at Condor Cycles.
Barry Scott at Bespoke.
Michel Lethenet at Mavic.
Cedric Chicken and Mike Catlin at Chicken Cycle Kit for Mavic wheels,
Campagnolo, Cinelli, Tifosi and Time bikes.
Joshua Riddle at Campagnolo.
And to Taz.

CONTENTS

01

THE ROAD BIKE

Whether you are an experienced racer or just starting out, knowing how to keep your bike in peak condition is essential to your enjoyment of cycling. Being able to recognise the early warning signs of mechanical trouble – and what to do about them – means less time and money wasted getting your bike fixed and more time in the saddle. Professional team bikes now cost in excess of £8,000 and, if you want the best, keeping a bike of this quality on the road is no easy task.

Whatever rider or mechanic level you are at, we hope that this clearly illustrated book with step-by-step photographs will help. It's fully up-to-date with the latest bikes and bike technology. In chapter 2 there are also some tips on what to look out for when buying a bike and some basic tool and workshop advice, should you need to start from scratch. Fixing a bike for yourself is hugely rewarding and it's great to know that you can be miles from home and yet be able to fix your bike in the unlikely event of a mechanical failure.

ROAD RACING BIKE

This is a road bike similar to the ones professional riders use. A bike with top-of-the-range components and lightweight wheels will cost the same as a hatchback car, although it requires far more looking after, and replacement parts and servicing can cost a fair bit. However, a perfectly balanced bike like this one will ride superbly. The component groupsets are usually Shimano Dura-Ace, SRAM Red or Campagnolo Super Record and wheels by Zipp, Mavic and

Lightweight are reassuringly expensive and very popular.

Road racing geometry is very aggressive and the position is quite extreme. Professional riders spend a long time in the saddle and are used to an aerodynamic position, so this will not be suited to a rider that only manages to ride a couple of times a week. Be realistic with your aspirations and consider a bike with a more 'Sportive' approach. Many manufacturers now offer high-end road bikes with the same technology and componentry as the professional's bike, albeit with a more relaxed fit and usually a more comfortable ride.

Many of these frames are ideal for long days in the saddle and riding over rough terrain and poor road surfaces. The pro teams sometimes use these bikes for Paris-Roubaix and the Tour of Flanders where they race for many hours over vicious cobbles and poor roads.

CYCLO-CROSS

Every winter, the sport of cyclo-cross means hundreds of road riders pull out their neglected 'cross bikes and head off-road. 'Cross bikes make an excellent second bike, as they can be set up as a commuter or training bike for the rest of the year.

A strong, lightweight, well-built frame is far more important than excellent components – once they're covered in mud, function level is pretty academic. Wheels and tyres also play a considerable part in cyclo-cross success. Many manufacturers now have a 'cross bike in their range, such is the current popularity of this winter sport. Once, these bikes would have been made up from old touring bikes and junk parts – now they're state-of-the-art carbon frames and high-end component-equipped race machines. Many mountain bike technologies have drifted into cyclo-cross including disc brakes and tubeless tyres, but cyclo-cross requires skill and control.

The Union Cyclist International (UCI – world cycling governing body) is very anxious to keep cyclo-cross pure and related to road bicycle riding as much as possible, so very often bikes that get too much like their mountain biking cousins are not allowed in sanctioned races. Cyclo-cross is a tough sport and teaches skill and technique that will help your road riding improve.

(See page 195 for more on cyclo-cross bikes.)

ENTRY-LEVEL RACING BIKE

An entry-level bike like this one will be mid-priced and perfect for your first few seasons of road riding, and even a race or two. Many of these bikes will have Compact Drive (see page 174), which is a good choice for beginners. Components-wise, look out for Shimano 105 or Campagnolo Veloce groupsets.

TOURING

Touring bikes are usually made from steel – it's not going to be the lightest bike on the market, but it will provide strength for carrying luggage and comfort for long rides. A long wheelbase and a steel fork are worth looking out for.

Some long-distance riders prefer a frame with slightly slacker seat and head tube angles, to provide a more comfortable ride. Often a custom-built bike is a good option so these characteristics are built into the bike. A custom fit is sometimes the best route for many of these riders, but there are several manufacturers now offering a more sedate road bike, perfect for all-day rides and challenge rides.

TRACK

Track bike geometry is generally tight and steep with short rake forks and a high bottom bracket (for pedal and banking clearance). Track bikes also have niche set-ups and types too – sprinters are after power so they prefer stiff, over-built frames with steel handlebars and lower front ends; endurance riders are after aerodynamics and usually use road components; and track pursuit bikes resemble road TT bikes.

Fixed-wheel competition track bikes have one drive option (fixed), no brakes and one gear ratio. Fixed has the main advantage of maintaining momentum (one of the reasons it's favoured by time-triallists and specialist hill-climbers). After riding fixed, your pedal action will become smoother (which is why track riders always have good pedal actions) and after thousands of kilometres you'll begin to use more of the pedal stroke to get the power down.

It's known as *souplesse* from the French – literally, a 'supple' pedal action. Riding a fixed bike on the road can be a wonderful experience too, but only if the riding in your area is suitable and you remember that you can't stop pedalling... so riding fixed can be hazardous if you're not familiar with fixed gear riding (it's best to go to the track to learn how) or the hardware you're using isn't up to the job. The climbing technique is also useful, as a single gear means you have to get up the hill in the only gear you have. It stops you getting lazy and using the gears, but it also teaches you how to squeeze every bit of advantage out of your technique – the momentum gained on the downstroke can easily be transferred to the upstroke, thus allowing all the power in the stroke to be used, and allowing a good pull technique to the stroke.

(See page 188 for more on Track bikes.)

SPORTIVE

It's not all about racing. Each year, several thousand riders take part in 'challenge rides'. These are often set out on one of the stages of the Grand Tours. You get to ride a stage of the Tour de France, known as the Etape, and some 10,000 participants are accepted each year with at least as many more being disappointed. Fancy being able to see what the professionals have to do for a living? You will not be disappointed – it's a very humbling experience. The bikes are often geared according to mountainous terrain and the fit is more relaxed and comfortable than a pure racing bike.

ROAD SINGLE SPEED

Fixed gears are also now popular again, not just for track racing but also for commuting and winter training. They're a sensible option too, as they don't wear out very easily and don't require new chains, cassettes and chainrings. Fitting two brakes is a good idea, although the joy of fixed is controlling your speed with the drivetrain, and many countries only require a front brake by law.

WINTER BIKE

The Northern European weather is hardly the ideal environment for bicycles. Winter bikes are often an entry-level bike or perhaps a retired racing bike. But seeing as most of your long training miles will be on this bike, a specialist bike with mudguards is the best way. Use the same set-up as your race bike, and similar contact points (saddle, bars, pedals), to prevent injury and discomfort.

TIME TRIAL

Time trials are the pivotal stages of big races like the Tour de France and the Giro d'Italia. Many professional teams will spend many hours testing products, frames and set-up to get every second out of the machine.

The essentials are a stiff, stable frame, aero TT handlebars and aero wheels. If you're taking your time trial riding seriously, you'll want to get a specific time trial bike. The differences between a standard road bike and a TT bike are not just aerodynamic.

A TT bike will have a steeper head- and seat-angle, thus placing the rider further forwards on the bike and into a more powerful pedalling position.

The frame may be smaller to allow the rider to get lower at the front of the bike. The wheelbase is shorter, and the overall result is a bike that is very responsive and twitchy, so it takes some getting used to. A TT bike may also be a little heavier than a standard road bike, as there are loads of extras added.

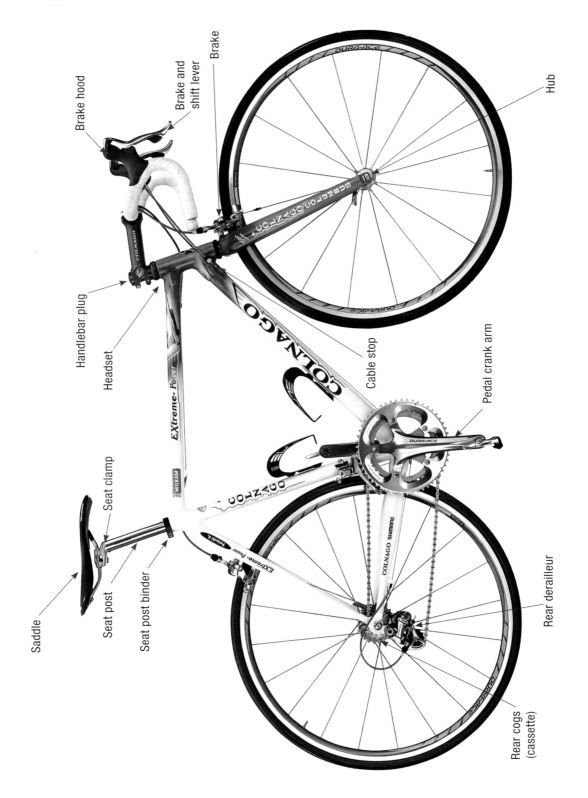

Brake hood

Brake and
shift lever

Brake

Hub

Handlebar plug

Headset

Cable stop

Pedal crank arm

Saddle

Seat clamp

Seat post

Seat post binder

Rear derailleur

Rear cogs
(cassette)

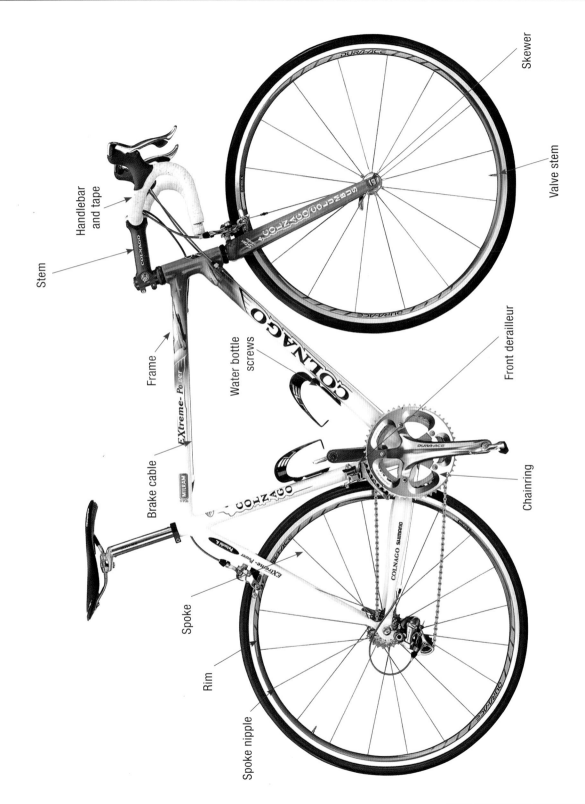

Skewer

Valve stem

Handlebar
and tape

Stem

Front derailleur

Frame

Water bottle
screws

Chainring

Brake cable

Spoke

Rim

Spoke nipple

BUYING A BIKE

Historically speaking, quality road bikes have always been built from the frame up. More recently, complete bikes from mainstream manufacturers have taken over as the preferred route for most riders. However, many quality bike shops offer the customer a better choice, with the possibility of customising the bike specification and building in personalised options. Complete bikes will, however, probably provide better value for the first-time buyer.

A new bike will come with full instructions for the consumer, details of any special parts (Shimano usually supplies instructions), a PDI (Pre-Delivery Inspection) checklist and, lastly, a warranty card. Any bike that can't supply this information should be avoided – you need to know you've done everything possible to prevent potential failures, which are very rare, but it's far better to use a bike that is up to the job in the first place. This information also signifies that a bike has been professionally assembled and checked from new, which is why your first port of call should be a quality local dealer.

Good entry-level road bikes usually cost around £500 to £800. Because this is a very competitive price point these bikes are often very good value, featuring quality parts and a well-made frame. However, entry-level bikes are not designed and built to be pushed to the limits, so as your riding improves you'll probably want to upgrade what you ride.

Remember that your main priorities are the frame and forks, then the wheels, then the contact points (saddle, handlebars and pedals), and lastly the components. Components are last on the list because they'll wear out in time and, should you want to upgrade them, you can do it when they wear out. The frame, forks and wheels are always the most expensive parts of a bike, so look for the manufacturers that put the most effort into these areas. Look for the details and workmanship to see that the manufacturer hasn't cut any corners.

TIPS FOR BUYING A BIKE

As with most things in life, there will be good and bad points about your new bike, but here are a few tips you should always consider before buying a new bike.

1 Take an experienced cycling friend with you to give you advice. Research the brands you like the look of. Phone the manufacturers for catalogues and take a balanced view, and use the internet – www.road.cc and www.roadbikereview.com both have user review sections, which can provide interesting insights.

2 Buy a range of up-to-date magazines to consider your options. Find back issues of group tests of bikes in your price range, or even e-mail the magazine to ask their opinion.

3 Find out each manufacturer's best sellers.

4 Ask these questions at each shop you visit:

- What size do I need and, if you haven't got one in that size, can you order it in? (See page 34 for more information on sizing.)
- Can I have a test ride? (See right for more information on test rides.)
- Do you provide a free first service?
- Within reason, can I swap parts (saddle, stem, handlebars and so on) to get the exact fit I want? The answer to all of these questions should be 'yes'.

5 Consider that you'll need after-sales support, so you'll need to build loyalty with the shop. Don't just buy cheaper elsewhere and then expect a local dealer to fix or deal with the warranty on your new bike for free. It's always worth thinking about buying some extras (helmet, clothing, tools and so on) when you're at the shop buying your bike. This is probably the most you'll spend in the shop at one time, so they may well offer you a few incentives, even if it's just a free bottle and an inner tube.

6 Don't be lured by discounted bikes, special offers or ex-demonstration bikes unless you're absolutely sure it's the bike for you and it's the right size.

7 If the shop doesn't have your size, wait until they can get one. It's better to leave it a little longer and have the right bike.

8 Always ask local cyclists for recommendations and ask them about the local shops – for example, which one is good for advice and which one specialises in particular brands? It's always better to go to a dealer who has a good reputation. Ask lots of questions in the shop and make sure they have a good mechanic and a well-equipped (preferably tidy) workshop. As discussed, they should also offer you a free first service and warranty back-up.

THE TEST RIDE

You may have to leave your credit card (or your car keys, other half, friend, dog, whatever) as security in the shop before they'll let you out on a test ride. When you leave the shop, relax and take the bike for a gentle spin. Stop somewhere quiet and have a good look over what you're about to buy. Try adjusting the saddle height so that you feel comfy. If you aren't happy, don't feel pressurised to buy – try something else instead.

SELF-BUILD BIKES

In time you may want to have a go at building your own bike. Frame-only deals can offer excellent value, but be aware that using second-hand or used parts can create problems as you build. Things like front mechs and seat posts often vary in size and, unless you have all the right tools, you can easily make an expensive mistake.

SECOND-HAND BIKES

Like self-build, buying a second-hand bike can be a bit of a hornet's nest. You may think you have a bargain, but if the bike has had any serious crash damage it could be a very bad move. Ideally, you should only buy a bike that has had little use.

If the drivetrain and brakes show signs of wear, the chances are that these parts are about to need replacing. If this is the case, you'll need to factor it into the bidding process, or reconsider the purchase if it will cost you more than the bike is worth to replace the worn-out parts. This is where taking an experienced riding friend is invaluable, as they'll be able to spot the telltale signs of misuse immediately. As with all second-hand purchases, be careful not to give out any personal details to people, unless you know who they are.

THE FRAME
GEOMETRY AND FRAME ANGLES

Whole books have been written on the subject of bicycle frame geometry – bike magazine articles, tests and features will provide much opinion on the subject too. What's here is an overview of road bike geometry, rather than an in-depth review. Good shops will have people with experience and sensible opinions, so ask around and be prepared with questions, so that you get the bike that suits you the best.

FRAME TYPES

The 'diamond pattern' frame with a front and rear triangle is still the most versatile approach for a bicycle frame.

Generally speaking, standard geometry (with a flat top tube parallel to the ground) allows for a more stable frame, and most experienced riders (and professionals) will prefer the predictable handling and comfort a standard geometry frame

will offer. Compact geometry refers to bikes with a sloping top tube that allows for a smaller rear triangle and, therefore, a slightly lighter frame. The result is a stiffer rear triangle but also, usually, a less forgiving ride.

FRAME ANGLES

Essentially you can have a seat or head angle that varies from 75–68 degrees (this is the angle measured behind the tube's centre line and the floor), so 75 degrees is steep and 68 degrees is slack.

HEAD TUBE ANGLE

This will play a major part in how the bike handles. A steep head angle will make the steering lighter and twitchy, yet at high speeds still quite stable for sprinting. A slacker head angle will provide stability at all speeds but heavier steering and a tendency to wallow a bit at sprinting speeds.

SEAT TUBE ANGLE

Seat angle has a major influence on your weight distribution and position over the pedals. It's a grey area, as saddle choice and seat post layback can also play a part in the overall picture. Time trial bikes usually have a steep seat angle to allow the rider to place themselves further forward, which provides a more powerful pedalling position and allows them to reach lower-set bars and triathlon-style armrests without a big stretch. A slacker angle is generally for a more relaxed rider and sometimes preferred by cyclo-cross riders, as they can force their weight further over the rear wheel to provide better traction in slippery conditions. However, don't compromise your fit for an over-slack or steep seat angle – fitting the bike accurately to your body is far more valuable.

Generally speaking (and depending on frame size), road bike manufacturers will go for a neutral 72–74 degree seat angle matched with a 71–73 degree head angle for a combination of comfort and stable, responsive handling.

FORK RAKE

Matching the fork rake to the head angle is essential, and forks have a variety of properties that influence the handling. Usually road racing forks have a 43mm rake (the distance from a centre line through the fork leg to the centre of the wheel hub) – track forks may be 37mm and touring forks as wide as 50mm. Shorter rake forks have a tendency to over-steer, i.e. turn a tighter cornering radius – longer raked forks will under-steer and have a wider turning circle.

Criterium racers prefer the former, and long-distance stage racers and challenge riders the latter. Most pro riders will opt for neutral handling to allow for comfort and improved control when descending, or riding over rough roads and cobblestones.

FRAME MATERIALS
STEEL

Generally, at entry level, there are sadly only a few steel frames available – sadly because, try as they might, the manufacturers can't make an aluminium frame with the same strength, longevity and ride characteristics. If you can, always buy a steel bike first – it will last you several years and can be used as a winter trainer if you buy a more expensive second bike later on. Reynolds, Deda, Columbus and True Temper make excellent steel tubing for bicycles, and steel doesn't have to be heavy either – Deda Zero One, Reynolds 953 and Columbus XCr are just as light as comparable Aluminium tubes. These days, 18lb (8.2kg) steel bikes are possible.

ALUMINIUM

Aluminium is the cheapest material to make bikes from, which is why the market is flooded with hundreds of different types and models. On the plus side this means they're very competitive and you can get a lot for a little money – however, on the downside they can be uncomfortably 'stiff' and are generally supplied in fewer sizes (often just Small, Medium and Large). So always remember to check the geometry before you buy, as some frames are made to very strange specifications.

The numbers quoted next to material relate to their alloy, with the 'T' suffix relating to the heat treatment e.g. 7075–T6. Steel-butted aluminium is stronger and lighter, and quality frames are heat-treated after welding to ensure maximum strength. Many cheap aluminium frames are neither butted nor heat-treated, so find out what a frame is made of and how it is made before you buy. Tubing from Deda, Easton and Columbus is at the quality end of this market. Aluminium is not always uncomfortable and is far more bicycle-friendly. Easton tubes can rightly claim to 'ride like steel'.

TITANIUM

Titanium is light, durable and can be a wonderful material to ride. However, it requires great skill to weld and therefore can be (and perhaps should be) expensive. It's the wonder material for bike-building – or so you might think. Sure, it's as light as aluminium, as strong as steel and as comfortable as an armchair, but... you have to be a very good framebuilder to build a good titanium bike – it's a very hard material to work with. So be very wary of cheap titanium frames, as there have been some horrendous bikes built in the past. Titanium is a high-end material, and as such should not be considered as a budget option, because you may have to compromise too much on the wheels and components with your available funds to get a decent frame.

CARBON FIBRE

Carbon fibre is fast establishing itself as the new material for frames. It's stiff, it's really light in weight, it can absorb vibration and it can flex, so it has excellent qualities for road bikes. Many aluminium bikes now have carbon sections too. Manufacturers have adopted carbon fibre as the current favoured frame material, and being light and strong it's easy to see why. However, there are better materials suited to riders who want long-term reliability and value for money.

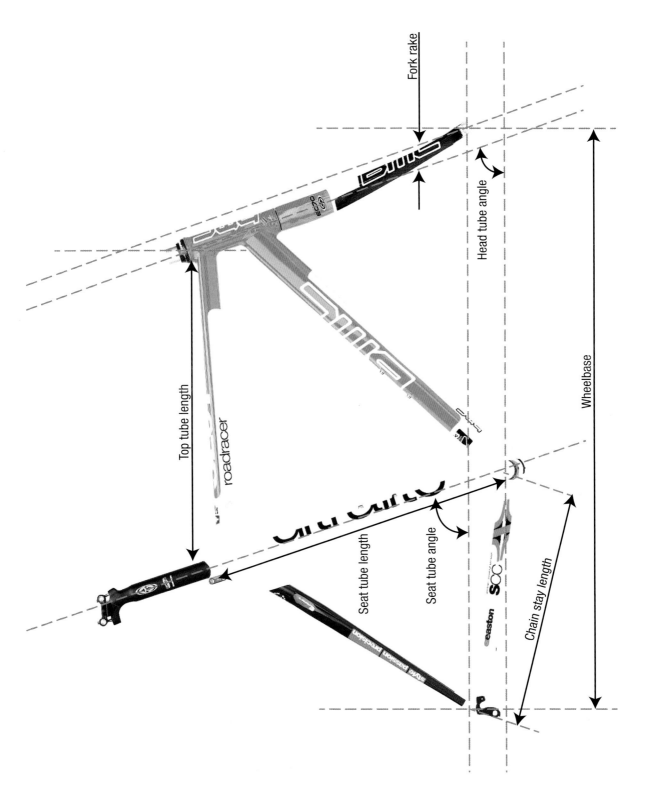

Fork rake

Head tube angle

Wheelbase

Top tube length

roadracer

Seat tube length

Seat tube angle

Chain stay length

FORK MATERIALS

Most forks are now made from carbon fibre – it soaks up road shock well and it's lightweight, strong and stiff. Carbon forks should always be checked out after a crash, and replaced should they show any signs of damage. Many mechanics recommend replacing well-used forks after two to three years, just to be safe.

Steel forks are still worth considering if you spend a long time in the saddle and/or you're of a heavy build yourself.

WHEELBASE

A short wheelbase makes handling quicker, and a compact rear triangle will provide stiffness, but at the expense of comfort. Super-short wheelbases were once very popular for racing, especially on very lightweight steel bikes, but are less so these days, as frames with aluminium and carbon with short wheelbases are a bit of a handful. Long wheelbases may take longer to get up to speed and require more effort to turn into corners, but they're super-comfortable and soak up the road shocks better.

If you don't want to race, a longer-wheelbase bike, perhaps with mudguard clearance, is a good choice.

FRAME MEASUREMENTS

Generally, frames are measured in centimetres and, annoyingly, the manufacturers have never come up with a standard industry method. Some measure from the centre of the bottom bracket to the top of the top tube ('centre-to-top' or 'C–T') and some to the

---

GENERAL MATERIALS APPLICATION GUIDE

- Cheap steel – entry-level, commuting and training bikes
- Expensive steel – touring, cyclo-cross, Audax and challenge-ride bikes
- Cheap aluminium – entry-level road bikes
- Expensive aluminium – racing bikes, specifically cyclo-cross, track and time-trial
- Titanium – comfortable race bikes and exotic road bikes
- Cheap carbon fibre – entry-level road-race bikes
- Expensive carbon fibre – road-race and weight-conscious riders

---

centre of the top tube ('centre-to-centre' or 'C–C'). So, knowing exactly what size you're buying (especially second-hand) can be a bit of a nightmare. However, most manufacturers measure the top tube in the same way – from the centre of the seat tube to the centre of the head tube – so this is usually a better way to reference frames. When it comes to bike fit, this top-tube measurement is very important. Seat-tube length can be easily adjusted (with the seat post) but it's not as easy to adjust the reach.

(For more on frame measurement, see the contact points section on pages 34-39.)

COMPONENTS

Much of this book is devoted to the fixing and adjustment of road components. I've used pretty standard groupsets and race-level components. However, there's a current trend for really lightweight (and really expensive) parts, which are interesting on a technology level but often require regular attention and servicing to keep them running. My advice to save your money is train harder

(and maybe lose weight) to go faster. Use reliable standard equipment rather than getting hung up on shaving grams from already lightweight stuff. Safety and reliability are paramount.

WHEELS

Personally I feel that the current lightweight racing wheels are not really appropriate for general riding and training, especially in the winter months when severe weather and road conditions don't favour sensitive components. Top-of-the-range wheels are designed with performance in mind, and you're far better off saving them for racing and sunny days. Wheels for everyday riding may be heavier, but a set of 32-hole standard wheels, if well built by a good wheelbuilder, will ride well and last far longer than factory-built super-lightweight performance wheels.

PEDALS AND CONTACT POINTS

Clipless pedals are safer and easier to use than standard toe clips and straps. Most entry-level road bikes now come supplied with clipless pedals.

02

THE HOME WORKSHOP

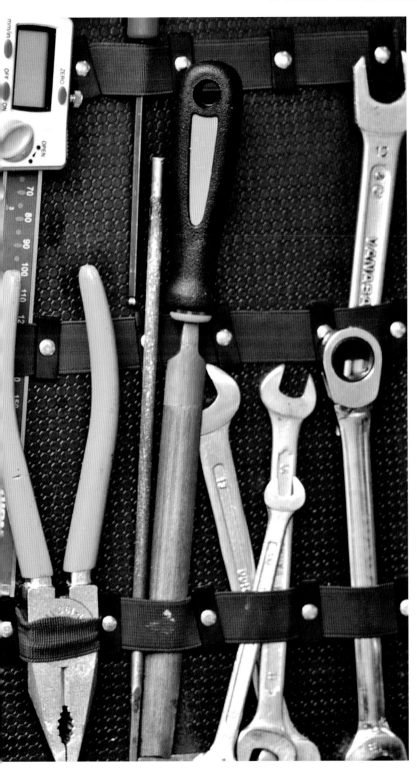

I've owned my fair share of bikes over the years and have collected a fairly comprehensive tool kit too. The bikes still come and go, but my tools should last a lifetime. This is why you should always buy good-quality tools, as you'll use them to fix lots of bikes. Specialist bike tools are expensive, but they make complicated procedures a breeze, and will also ensure you don't damage your new components and your bike or hurt yourself. Bodging jobs with cheap tools only ends in compromise, and if you have a good-quality bike it deserves the tools to complement it.

WORKSHOP TOOL KIT

For a modest outlay you can cover most home workshop jobs. Frame tools, specialist tools and cutting tools do cost a fair amount, but in time you will consider them a worthwhile investment. In the meantime, the best advice is to buy components from a local shop and get their mechanic to fit them for you if you don't have the tools yourself.

However, as you become a more competent mechanic you may want to consider how much you spend in the bike workshop compared to how much the tools will cost you.

MORE ADVANCED HOME TOOLS

As you become more experienced and your confidence increases, consider adding the following items to your workshop tool kit:

- Headset press

- Headset cup remover

- Crown race remover

- Crown race setting tool

- Rear mech hanger straightening tool

- Set of taps for threads

- Rear dropout alignment tools

- Steerer cutting guide

BASIC TOOLS

- Allen keys: 1.5mm, 2mm, 2.5mm, 3mm, 4mm, 5mm, 6mm, 8mm and 10mm are the sizes most often used

- Track pump

- Chain cleaner

- Cleaning brushes

- Pliers (flat and needle nose)

- Cable cutters

- Screwdrivers (small and large; flat and cross-head)

- Nylon hammer (or mallet) and ball-peen (metal-working) hammer

- A set of metric, open-ended spanners from 6mm to 24mm

- Cassette lock ring tool

- Chain whip

- Chain tool

- Cable puller

- 'Podger' (sharp-ended tool like a bradawl)

- Star nut-setting tool

- Adjustable spanner

- Cone spanners (17mm, 15mm and 13mm)

- Pedal spanner

- Workshop-quality chain tool

- Chain checker (for measuring chain wear)

- Torque wrenches

- Crank-removing tool

- Bottom bracket tools

- Headset spanners (optional)

- Wheel-truing stand

- Spoke keys

- Hacksaw (standard and junior)

- Files (flat and half-round)

- Socket set

ADVANCED AND PROFESSIONAL WORKSHOP TOOLS

- Head tube reamer and facing kit

- Bottom bracket tapping and facing kit

- Fork crown facing kit

- Seat tube reamer

- Frame alignment tool

- Chainline gauge

- Wheel dishing stick

- Spoke tension meter

THE TOOLS

1   Tool box
2   Long-nose pliers
3   Allen keys
4   Chainring nut spanner
5   Chain tool
6   Screw drivers

7   Chain whip
8   Pedal spanner
9   Cone spanners
10 Chain wear tool
11 Crank remover
12 Adjustable spanner
13 Cassette tool
14 Cable cutters

15 Tyre levers
16 Wheel jig
17 Crank bolt spanner
18 Torque wrench
19 Multi-tool
20 Shimano Bottom
    Bracket tool
21 Star-fangled nut setter

22 Crank remover
23 Cassette tool
24 Cable puller
25 Spanner
26 Headset spanners
27 Cable pliers
28 Soft mallet

WORKSHOP SET-UP

A home workshop is a bit of a luxury, but fixing your bike in the kitchen is never a great idea. So here are some tips for setting up your workshop at home.

HOW YOU WORK

A stable workstand (below) is essential. The best workshop type will be fixed to a wall or a solid workbench, so jobs that require bashing or heavy leaning won't make the stand move around the floor as you 'dance' with your bike.

A solid workbench makes tough jobs like fitting headset parts or cutting down fork steerers easy. A tool board helps you find tools quickly, and quality tools should be stored in a toolbox especially if your workshop is damp. You can also assemble an 'in the field' toolbox

that you can take with you to races or rides so you can fix emergencies in the car park.

SPILLS

Put down a mat for spillages. Remember that if you have to fix your bike in the kitchen, you'll need something on the floor to soak up the mess. Workshop mats are readily available from bike or tool shops. They also keep your feet warm in the winter.

SECURITY

Hooks and lockable anchor points are a good idea, just in case you're broken into. Storing your bike(s) like this also prevents them from falling over and getting scratched by the lawn mower.

WORKSHOP PRACTICES
HEALTH AND SAFETY WARNING

Lubricants, disc-brake fluid, degreasers and bike washes

look after your bike well enough, but they can be very harmful to your skin – always read the instructions and labels on cans before you start work. Take care and use appropriate PPE (Personal Protective Equipment) when working on your bike. Latex or Nitrile gloves and workshop aprons are a great idea and safety glasses are a must when using release agents or operating grinders and drills. Using the right tools helps too (see right for more information).

READ THE INSTRUCTIONS

This may seem obvious, but it's very important. Warranties and guarantees are only any good if you install things correctly. Even the simplest of components will have some recommendations from the manufacturer – so stick to them. Use the recommended tools and torque settings.

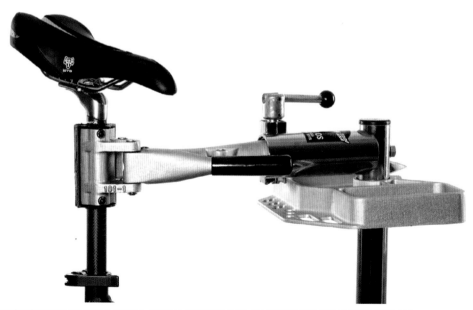

A QUALITY WORKSTAND IS ESSENTIAL FOR ALL REPAIRS AND SERVICING. ALL BIKE MECHANICS SHOULD OWN ONE

A BENCH-MOUNTED VICE. THIS ONE HAS SOFT JAWS TO HOLD THINGS SECURELY BUT WITHOUT DAMAGING THEM

If in doubt, contact the shop or the manufacturer. Don't make expensive mistakes.

TOOLS AND EQUIPMENT
THE VICE
The vice (left) needs to be properly bolted and secured to the solid workbench. A vice is essential for hub and headset jobs, and a pair of replaceable 'soft jaws' for the vice will help to protect valuable and sensitive components.

WHEEL JIG
Your wheel jig (see over) should preferably be bench-mounted. A solid wheel jig makes truing wheels far easier. If you intend to learn how to build wheels, or just want to get better at home truing, then a wheel jig is a must-have item.

POWER TOOLS
An electric drill will help with frame repairs and removing seized pedal cleat bolts, and a bench-mounted grinder is useful for repairs and customising components. Care must be taken to wear the right PPE (see workshop practices) when working.

TORQUE WRENCHES
Torque wrenches (Park Tools version, left) take the guesswork out of assembling aeroplanes, car engines and machines, and enable engineers to fasten bolts to manufacturers' recommended figures, so they're great for bikes too. They're simple to use – set the level on the screw gauge on the handle, shown in Newton

LARGE TORQUE WRENCHES ARE ESSENTIAL FOR INSTALLING CRANKS CORRECTLY

EVEN PROFESSIONAL MECHANICS IMPROVISE AT THE RACES. THIS WHEEL TRUING STAND IS PORTABLE AND INEXPENSIVE

TORQUE WRENCHES COME IN A VARIETY OF SIZES – THE SMALL SIZE IS PERFECT FOR MOST JOBS BUT A BIGGER WRENCH IS NEEDED FOR BOTTOM BRACKET REPLACEMENT OR SOME CRANK AND PEDAL JOBS

TRAVELLING TOOL TIPS

1 Spokes can be taped to a frame tube or hidden in the seat post.

2 Cable spokes are handy for quick repairs and, as they hook into the spoke holes rather than having to be pushed through – you don't have to remove the cassette to repair it.

3 Always leave your ride tool kit intact and keep it just for riding. Taking tools out to fix your bike at home will mean you'll leave your tyre levers on the kitchen table and not have them when you really need them...

4 Carry a spoke key on your keyring – this makes your keys easier to find too!

5 Tool kits can be stuffed into old drink bottles and placed in a spare bottle cage. Make sure it can't rattle out by securing it with a toe strap.

6 If you're riding with friends, spread the big tools around – don't all carry the same stuff.

7 Always carry a folding set of Allen keys, with a small screwdriver too, tyre levers, a tube or two and a set of emergency patches. A saddle pack will carry this basic kit. For longer rides, you might want to add a chain tool, a spoke key, a small spanner and some minor spares, such as brake pads and chain links.

metres (Nm), then add the correct Allen or bolt head (they have either a 3/8 inch or 1/8 inch socket drive) and tighten the bolt until the handle 'gives' with a click. This type is perfect for most Allen bolts on a bike.

Park Tools' version of the torque wrench has a beam, which 'bends' when the handle is balanced, allowing you to read off the torque on the dial. You'll need a bigger one like this (see previous page) for cassette lock rings, cranks and bottom brackets. On road bikes it's important to use recommended torque settings, for warranty reasons and for safety – especially on suspension forks and disc brakes with many moving parts and fastenings. All well-trained mechanics will use a torque wrench – don't build a bike up without one.

TRACK PUMP

A track pump will set tyre pressures quickly and accurately and is far better than a mini pump. However, some pressure gauges are more reliable than others, so get a separate, accurate tyre-pressure gauge too.

A SELECTION OF LUBES AND GREASES – SEVERAL ARE NEEDED FOR DIFFERENT MATERIAL APPLICATIONS

GREASE

You'll develop preferences for particular brands of lubes and greases, but the modern bicycle requires a selection of advanced lubricants to keep it running sweetly:

- Ti-prep (or copper slip) – a grease with tiny copper flakes in it, which prevents titanium and alloys from seizing – must be used on all titanium threads.

- Anti-seize grease – this is for large threads and components that stay put for long periods (seat posts, bottom bracket threads, headset cups and pedal threads).

- PTFE (Teflon)-based light dry lube – this is preferred for summer use and assemblies like mechs and brake calliper pivots.

- Heavy wet lube – this is best for wet weather as it's harder to wash away than dry lube.

- Silicone greases – use these for intricate moving parts like pedal and hub bearings.

- Waterproof greases – use these for components that get ignored for long periods like Aheadset bearings.

- Degreaser – used for cleaning moving parts and components that get bunged up with muck.

- Bike wash – use it for tyres, frame tubes and saddles.

- Release agent – this is good for removing seized seat-posts and stubborn bottom brackets. Be careful, as it can ruin your paintwork.

THE BASICS

Once you've bought a bike, it should be properly prepared and checked over by the shop mechanic (pre-delivery inspection or 'PDI'). You might be asked about any personal set-up preferences, and the mechanic will ensure that the gears and brakes are properly adjusted. So, in theory, your bike will be ready for the road.

But you need to be sure that the bike is right for you in the first place, and isn't an impulse buy that is totally unsuited to your body shape or type of riding you intend to do.

This aside, after you get home you'll still need to tweak things to get the bike just right for you, and you'll need to keep everything maintained and running sweetly, even if the shop are offering you a free first service as part of the deal. This chapter outlines what you need to know to keep you and your bike on the road without expensive mishaps.

POSITION – CONTACT POINTS, SITTING AND STEERING

SIZING

As I mentioned in the buyers' guide on pages 8-13, most reputable bike dealers will be able to help you pick the right-sized bike. As with most large purchases, it's worth getting a few opinions. For the standard road-riding position, you're looking for comfort first and foremost, so feeling relaxed and being able to move freely are essential. Remember – a bike needs to be an extension of your body, so it must fit perfectly. Above all, you must be honest about your aspirations and your physical shape. So, if you're just about to rush out and spend several thousand pounds on your pride and joy, just wait a minute and consider the following questions:

- Is the bike right for your type of riding – does it fulfil your aspirations and is it right for the kind of riding you do?
- Are you in the right shape and proportion to ride in the position that you've set your bike up in?
- Does anything hurt (other than your legs from the effort) when you ride your bike?

The answers to these questions might well tell you that you've bought a bike based on passion or style, rather than function. It may also mean that you're not in the finest physical shape to get the most out of it and that it hurts like hell after a few hours' riding...

Professional bike riders are a fastidious lot. The great Eddy Merckx was so fussy about his saddle height that he often carried a saddle-spanner when racing, and even adjusted it 'on the fly' when descending mountains. Nothing much has changed – pro riders today are still very particular about their bike's set-up.

Another important thing to consider is that pro bike riders are so professional in their approach because they're extremely talented athletes who want to use their skills to the max. To make it into the pro peloton you have to be able to ride a bike very fast and for a very long time. And that isn't easy.

Flexibility and the physical ability required to ride 35,000–40,000km (22,000–25,000mi) a year means that the bike set-up for a pro rider is never going to be suitable for someone who rides a fraction of that distance, and can barely touch their toes. So be realistic about the bike you ride – in reality it might be slowing you down.

BIKE SET-UP

There's only so much tinkering with saddle heights that you can do yourself, and at the very least an experienced rider should be able to help you set up a bike, if not a pro. Professional bike-fitting and analysis are now very popular and readily available, so get an appointment. Physiologists can study your movement on the bike too, and a trained bike-fitter will have experience of a variety of body types and riding aspirations, so they're well worth a visit. Basically what I'm saying here is don't guess at it, especially before you spend a pile of money on the wrong-sized frame.

ADAPTATION

It takes a few weeks to adapt to a new bike set-up. This is why experienced riders will only adjust saddle height and pedal cleats by very small increments, so that their body doesn't experience any 'aftershock' from big changes in set-up. For this reason you must try to stick with one set-up as much as possible to avoid injury and to make sure your muscles are used to their way of riding.

It's not easy to copy exactly the same set-up without having identical bikes, but try and keep it as close as possible.

SADDLE HEIGHT

Former World Road Race Champion Tom Boonen once stated that he found his ideal saddle height completely by mistake. His seat post slipped 20mm and he found the position more powerful and more comfortable than his previous 'correctly calculated' saddle height. These things are peculiar to the individual and many scientific studies have shown there are certain instances where 'feel' and experience alter the set-up.

Computer-fits and multiplying your inside leg measurement will only get you into the ballpark – dialling the height perfectly will take much longer. To assess your current position, you can do several things yourself.

1 Video yourself during a turbo training session, as this shows any abnormalities and problems as they happen. Get a (patient) friend to do the filming and then they can concentrate on different parts of your body for a few minutes or so. Note how you revert to your worst habits as the session increases in intensity. Your trunk (torso) may begin to roll from side to side, the shoulders can start to rock and you may over-reach for the pedals as your hips start to rock from side to side. It's also likely that you'll shift further and further forwards (or backwards) in the saddle too. Other things to look out for are

pedalling style and foot-orientation. See how you can adapt the bike to counter these habits – perhaps a lower or higher saddle, or a shorter stem.

2 Look at your handlebar tape. Where is it most worn away? Where do you spend most of your riding time? Most riders' hands will be on the tops of the bars on the lever hoods for quick access to the brakes and gears. If you find you ride most of the time with outstretched arms and your fingers just touching the bars, it's highly likely your bike is too long.

3 Take a good look at how your bike is set up before you start to adjust the components. Measure and make a record of the following critical dimensions:

- Bar/saddle drop: Use a long level or get a broom handle (it has to

be dead straight) and measure the drop from the saddle to the centre of the handle-bar. (Ignore pro bike set-up for a moment.) This should be no greater than 10cm, and preferably a lot less. You're aiming to get the saddle and bars as close as possible to level.

- Distance between the tip of the saddle to the centre of the handlebar (or end of the stem) is defined by your trunk-length, arm-reach and arm-length, but it can vary enormously depending on bar and component manufacturer.

- Measure from the centre of the saddle rail to the centre of the bottom bracket (your saddle height)

- Also measure: crank lengths; bar type, width, reach and drop; and stem length.

30MM OF SPACERS CAN BE PLACED UNDER THE STEM – ANY MORE MAY MEAN THAT THE STEM NEEDS TO BE CHANGED FOR A DIFFERENT ANGLE

THE SADDLE SHOULD BE DEAD LEVEL, NOT SLOPING BACK OR FORWARD

MEASUREMENTS ARE TAKEN FROM THE CENTRE OF THE BOTTOM BRACKET AXLE

SETTING SADDLE HEIGHT

There are many techniques for determining the correct saddle height, and generally speaking you only have a small 'zone' of leg extension – i.e. the difference between too high and too low is minimal. You're aiming to make sure hips remain as still as possible. When the hips rock from side to side you can say that the saddle is too high (see 'leg-length discrepancy' and 'postural problems' below for more details).

BAR HEIGHT

Are your handlebars too low? This is the current trend in road bikes. The Aheadset has meant that the stem ends up low on the head tube and this in turn adds extra distance between the saddle and the stem. The result of low bars is usually a pain in the neck from having to crane your head/neck forwards.

OTHER FACTORS

It's not just bike-fit – these are the other main issues and influences on bike comfort:

BEER BELLY?

A fat tummy will stop you reaching lower, as your legs have to travel around your rotundness on every up-stroke of the pedal revolution, reaching lower (or further away) for the bars simply amplifies this. This is why larger riders ride with a very 'knees-open' pedal-stroke, and not only will your extra weight slow you down on the hills, it also makes for a very inefficient pedalling pattern. Therefore many overweight riders will suffer knee and joint issues as a result.

CHECKING SADDLE HEIGHT FROM THE CENTRE OF THE BOTTOM BRACKET AXLE

POOR FLEXIBILITY

Cyclists are notoriously bad at stretching – it's by far the easiest way to avoid injury and postural problems.

MUSCLE WEAKNESS, IMBALANCE OR INJURY

Physiotherapy or osteopathy may be required, followed by core-strength training and a supplementary training or rehabilitation programme.

PREVIOUS INJURIES

Again, it's worth a trip to a qualified doctor to check that any old war wounds won't come back with your new bike set-up.

SUDDEN DAMAGE

Crashes or accidents can severely compromise your set-up if you don't check carefully for damage.

CONGENITAL ISSUES

How you sit on a bike can only be changed so much. It's possible that you have an untypical body-shape, and this may mean you need a custom-built frame.

POSTURAL PROBLEMS

Sitting all day or standing all day will place differing strains and impact on your body. Cycling is weight-bearing, so there isn't much strain on the body, but there can be if the position has been poorly matched somewhere.

LEG-LENGTH DISCREPANCY

A leg-length discrepancy can be due to a hip or back problem that is amplified by countless hours on the bike. Again, see a qualified doctor or expert.

PEDALS AND PEDAL ALIGNMENT

There are dozens of different pedal systems and all have their benefits. Clipless pedals are used by most cyclists these days, although some track sprinters will still use toe straps to make sure that they stay in touch with the bike when wrenching the cranks with enormous force. Pedal cleats need to be regularly checked for wear and for twisting, so the bolts need to be tight and constantly checked. Worn cleats can rock from side to side, prevent the float from working effectively and also disengage unexpectedly. The feet need to be stable too – rocking feet use up energy and also can play havoc with ankle, knee and hip joints.

CLEAT FITTING – FORE AND AFT
Just for a moment, go to the foot of a staircase. Try to climb the stairs with flat feet. Hard isn't it? The human body is designed to 'climb' on the balls of the feet, so this way you're using all your leg muscles to the best of their capability. So for this reason the centre of the ball of your foot should be placed directly over the centre of the pedal axle. This will mean all your leg's power can be 'expressed' into the drivetrain.

ORTHOTICS AND SHIMS
Cleats can be wedged and orthotic inserts made for shoes to correct your foot plant and also help the pedal-stroke. This can also align the joints, and solve pedalling inefficiency and stroke abnormalities, sometimes instantly. This is a pretty new science to cycling, but in the same way it affects runners with shoe choice, your foot plant also affects your cycling. A podiatrist may be able to help in the first instance. Specialized Body Geometry shoes have also started to address the issues here too.

FIT SPECIFICS
So far most of this information has been specifically for road

bikes, but here are the main influences on set-up for different disciplines.

CLIMBING
The climbing position is usually more upright, and Tour de France riders will often lengthen their stem to allow them to pull further forwards on the bars on the long ascents and open up the lungs for deeper breathing.

CYCLO-CROSS
Again, a slightly higher bar position may mean that the saddle needs to be raised slightly too, although most 'cross riders adopt a similar position to their road bike's. The bars are also better closer to you, usually by fitting a shorter stem, as this position provides better slow-speed control and faster steering. 'Cross riders usually work hard on their technique, and therefore the bike set-up will be tweaked to gain the best combination of slow-speed handling and comfort before flat-out aerodynamic road speed.

TIME TRIALS (TT)
Opinions on aerodynamics in cycling are very involved. One thing that everyone agrees on, however, is that the best way to go faster is to use the most aerodynamic, yet still comfortable, position you can. This should come before you start to worry about disc wheels, aero helmets and expensive machinery. In fact there's plenty of evidence to suggest that a properly set-up TT bike with standard wheels and equipment is far quicker than a

badly set-up aero TT bike with the latest kit on it. If you're very keen on time trials and want to improve, get comfortable first and foremost, but also be scientific. Experiment with your position and use a power crank to see which position works best for you. Get a bike-fitter to look at your position, and don't just throw a bike together and think that just because it looks right, it is right. (See page 198 for more on TT set-up.)

TRACK
On the track, power is the key element, even over comfort, although many endurance track riders (who are usually road riders as well) adopt the same

---

WOMEN'S FIT

Women's bikes are designed specifically to suit the female physique. In general terms, women tend to have a shorter body and longer legs, proportionally, than men. This means that a long top tube will have to be countered with an upright seat post without any layback and a shorter stem.

It is even better to have a shorter top tube too, which is why there are so many brands that have a specific women's bike in their range. Women's saddles are wider to offer more support, and handlebars can be narrower to account for narrower shoulders. Again, spend time with the shop staff and get the bike comfortable – ensure you're happy before you leave the shop.

position on all of their bikes. The common mistake is to raise the saddle height in the quest for more power, when the opposite is actually the true way towards a more powerful position, as it allows you to recruit more muscle power into the pedal stroke.

For the sprinters, bar height and reach are usually lower for aerodynamics, but you're less likely to use the top part of the bars (unless riding the Madison), so this should be considered when settling on a position. Sprinters travel at speeds of over 80kmh (50mph), so control is also important. Don't be tempted just to fit a negative rise stem and the deepest set of drops you can find, experiment with your sprinting position instead.

Currently, sprinters are opening up the position and raising the bars so they can actually fill their lungs more easily and be able to bend the arms more to reach the lower tuck position. Too long and low means that the arms are too straight, and this is no good for match sprinting where the riders throw the bike all over the place.

FIT SPECIFICS OVERVIEW

The following is only a guide and, as everybody is an individual, please make sure you seek personal advice from an experienced bike-fitter.

1   Start with the saddle flat. If you feel that the saddle needs to be tilted nose-down it may mean you have the saddle too high. Pointing the nose up will create all sorts of problems and discomfort on long rides.

2   For reach, your arms should be comfortably bent and the saddle-to-bar drop should allow you to sit with a relatively straight back. A shorter handlebar stem will quicken the steering but not necessarily improve control, but being too cramped can prevent you from shifting your weight across the saddle.

3   Correct saddle height is interpreted in a variety of ways. The general consensus is that your leg should be slightly bent at the bottom of the pedal stroke, without your hips having to sway on the saddle to perform the stroke. But this is open to interpretation, so have an experienced fitter check your saddle height.

4   Much of bike-fit fine-tuning can be done by exchanging components such as the saddle and stem. Test-ride the bike after each change and make sure you're happy with the set-up before you leave the shop.

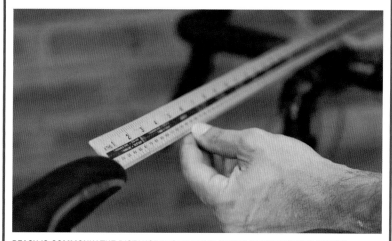

REACH IS COMMONLY THE DISTANCE FROM THE TIP OF THE SADDLE TO THE CENTRE OF THE HANDLEBAR

FINDING THE RIGHT RIDING POSITION

The wrong riding position can cause you all sorts of problems, in particular a bad back. Here are some suggestions to help you get it right – get a friend to help you, take photographs or use a full-length mirror to help you get the best balanced position.

SADDLE HEIGHT
TOO LOW

This will place excessive strain on the knees. Track riders and time triallists often ride lower to achieve maximum power – however, a balanced road riding position is usually for long periods in the saddle, so too low can create problems.

TOO HIGH

The rider will have to stretch to reach the pedals at the bottom of each stroke, which tilts the pelvis and pulls on the lower back muscles. The same principle applies if you bob back and forth excessively when riding hard.

ABOUT RIGHT

The knee should be slightly bent at the bottom of the pedal stroke. An easy way to judge this is to have the heel of your foot on the pedal with your leg fully extended at the bottom of the stroke, then pedal backwards. If you find that you rock from side to side excessively, your saddle is too high and you need to reset it so that you feel smooth in this position. This way, when the ball of your foot is placed on the pedal there will be a bit of extra slack built into your saddle height.

Alter your saddle height by small increments of no more than 5mm at a time and give yourself a few weeks to get used to it. That's why it's best to change position during the winter months, as you won't be riding as regularly.

STEM FORE/AFT POSITION
TOO CRAMPED

This will make you arch your back and stress the lower muscles. It also means you ride with your weight further forwards, which will make the steering sluggish.

TOO STRETCHED

This usually forces you to lock out your arms and strain your neck to see ahead, both of which will contribute towards lower back pain. The handling will feel sketchy and a bit too light.

ABOUT RIGHT

A balanced position means that you'll be able to stretch out comfortably and bend your arms to assist in shock absorption. With the stem in the right position, your weight will be better distributed over the bike.

SADDLE FORE/AFT POSITION
TOO FAR BACK

This is good for climbing power and pedalling comfort over a long ride, but places extra strain on neck, arm and shoulder muscles.

TOO FAR FORWARDS

You'll get a lot of pedal power in this position, but it places a lot of stress on the larger muscles, and can cause fatigue and tightness in the upper leg.

ABOUT RIGHT

You should be able to pass a vertical line (use a bit of string and a weight for a plumb line) through the centre of your knee (the bony lump just behind your kneecap) and the pedal spindle when the cranks are parallel to the ground.

REMOVING WHEELS

The quick-release lever (or QR) was invented by the Italian engineer and racer Tuilio Campagnolo. In the days when he was racing, the riders had to stop to change gear on their fixed-wheel bikes, swapping the wheel around for the other side of the hub where a lower gear sprocket was fitted. Racing in the Dolomites one cold day and over

the Croce d'Aune pass, with his hands freezing, he couldn't undo the wing nuts that held his wheel in place – legend has it that he invented the quick-release lever as a result of this hardship.

These days, the standard road-bike wheel has a QR mechanism which is essentially the same design as the one Mr Campagnolo invented. This system is excellent for removing the wheels instantly, which is great for repairing punctures, quick racing-wheel

changes, or putting your bike in the back of your car.

But, to the uninitiated, a QR mechanism can be potentially hazardous if done up incorrectly. On most bikes the front-wheel system has a slightly different technique from the rear-wheel system. If you're removing both wheels, take the front one out first – this will make the bike easier to manage and means that you won't have to drag the chain and gears on the ground.

FRONT WHEELS

1 'Lawyer tabs' are so called because of several well-publicised US lawsuits in the early days of the mountain bike, when a few companies were sued over front wheels dropping out of the forks unannounced, which had catastrophic results. They're designed to prevent the wheel from falling out should the QR lever be done up too loosely (see box, right).

2 Once the QR is undone the wheel may still not drop out completely, so the nut on the non-lever side needs to be loosened a little more. The key here is to remember how much you've undone it and not to remove

it completely. To clear the tabs, undo the nut – three full turns will be enough on most bikes. The wheel will then drop out.

3 The springs on the inside of the QR mechanism help centralise the nut and the lever to push them away from the bike. They also make it easier to replace the wheel, as you

don't have to centre the assembly. This leaves your hands free to hold the bike and position the wheel into the fork ends.

4 The front wheel has to be firmly placed into the dropouts before you can do up the lever. For this reason I suggest you replace the wheels with the bike on the ground – this way the weight of the bike can help make the wheels go in straight. It's best to do the levers up when the weight of the bike is on the wheels. You can lean over and do the front wheel up this way.

REAR WHEELS

1 The chain should be on the smallest sprocket (or cog) and the largest chain ring, so make sure you change into this gear before you start. This makes it easier to get the chain off the cassette and easier to replace the wheel afterwards.

2 Stand behind the bike and hold the bike upright with your legs trapping the wheel, leaving your hands free to remove the wheel. Now undo the lever.

3 The wheel will remain trapped into the bike by the chain, so twist the mech backwards to release the wheel. The chain should stay on the front chain wheel, so it'll be easier if you start with the chain in this position when you replace the wheel. The wheel will now easily come out of the rear triangle.

4 To replace the rear wheel, the mech needs to be sprung into the correct position with the wheel in the bike. Next, wrap the chain over the top of the smallest sprocket to help the wheel slot into the dropouts.

5 Pull the wheel upwards and backwards, and it should slot into place easily. If it doesn't, the wheel may have become snagged on the brake pads, or the mech may not be in the correct gear position.

6 Don't adjust the nut on the QR lever, as the rear wheel should clear the dropouts and slip in easily. However, it's worth checking that the lever feels tight as it closes. Rest your weight on the bike, as this will keep the wheel central in the rear dropouts.

LAWYER TABS – MADE FOR SAFETY, NOT FOR SPEED

The rather aptly named Lawyer tabs are two small stubs of material on the fork ends that prevent the wheel from dropping out should the quick release come undone while riding. Although on a road bike this is highly unlikely, they were added first to mountain bikes, where you are more likely to lift the front wheel to clear obstacles. As their name suggests, they were added as a result of a few nasty accidents and large legal bills for manufacturers. Previously on road bikes they were added and pro mechanics would file them off, because in order to remove the wheel the skewer must be undone slightly to clear the tabs and allow the wheel to drop out. The UCI decided that this would be illegal as of the start of the 2013 season. It's an on-going debate, needless to say wheel changes take longer and it's more to do with the rule that nothing on the bike can be changed - but I suspect it has more to do with litigation than it does with common sense.

DOING UP THE QR LEVER
(BOTH WHEELS)

1 Once the wheel is slotted into the dropouts (or fork ends), slowly tighten the nut up until the lever starts to tighten. When the lever is directly in line with the skewer as shown here that is enough – this will ensure that the lever will close tightly enough.

2 The lever needs to start to tighten in this position – this is when the cam on the mechanism begins to 'bite' and when the wheel hub is gripped across the lock nuts and by the fork ends.

3 It should close firmly, needing enough effort so that you have to use your thumb and press hard. Any harder and you'll struggle to undo it again. Check that the wheel spins centrally in the forks or rear stays and you're safe to ride.

IMPORTANT! TIGHTENING THE QUICK RELEASE

Tightening the QR adequately is essential for safety and this needs to be checked regularly, especially before and after rides. Also, be careful where you position the lever in the closed position. Place the front QR so that it runs behind the fork, and the rear one in line with the seat stay (pointing towards the saddle). This will also make it easier to undo the lever in a hurry.

TRANSPORTING YOUR BIKE

You have several options for transporting your bike – in your car, on a boot rack, on a roof rack or in a travel bag. Some are better than others…

IN YOUR CAR

The safest way to carry your bike is in the back of your car. Remove both the wheels (see pages 40-42) and then wrap the chain and rear mech in a cloth so as not to get oil all over the place.

Try to pack your bike last and on top of all your other kit, and lay the wheels under the frame. It's a good idea to get some wheel bags (bin liners are good too), especially if it's been wet. Try not to let the tyres rub on anything sharp, or you'll have a nasty shock when the sidewalls wear a hole and puncture.

ON A ROOF RACK

Remove all loose-fitting equipment, such as drink bottles, tool packs, pumps and so on. Fasten the front wheel into the wheel clamp. Give the fork leg a good shake to ensure it's tight. Fasten the rear wheel strap and you're set. Before you drive off, double-check that all the straps are tight and you haven't left anything on the ground around the car or on top of the roof.

If you stop for anything, lock the bikes to the rack (most racks now have lockable fork fastenings) and always use a roof rack with lockable roof brackets. Lastly, don't go into a supermarket or height-limited car park, as this will ruin

your bike, car and roof rack. And yes, it does happen more often than you might think!

ON A BOOT RACK

Boot racks are not ideal. Many retro-fit to the car with straps and rest on bumpers and rear windows, and are therefore not suited to carrying heavy bikes or more than two. They scratch your car and can, in time, damage the rear windows. The best type of boot rack is one that fits to the tow bar or is a permanent fitting.

IN A TRAVEL BAG OR BOX

1 First, remove the pedals, saddle and seat post. Wrap these up in a jiffy bag and place them straight into the bag or into your hand luggage – don't leave them on the kitchen table.

2 Remove the wheels and take out the QR skewers. It's worth letting the tyres down almost completely –

they shouldn't explode in the hold, but it's better to be safe. I leave a little air in just to protect the rims and to provide some more padding.

3 Cover the ends of the axle with cardboard to prevent them causing any damage inside the bag. Better still, use the plastic axle covers that the wheels are supplied with (a local bike shop should have a good supply).

4 Preferably place the wheels in the bag or box and tape them to one another at the rim, or use electrical zip ties. Space them so that the cassette and axle won't damage the frame. Better still, put them in padded wheel bags too to prevent any damage to the spokes.

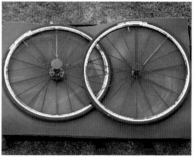

5 If you're using a padded bag, remove the rear mech, as it's vulnerable and is one less thing to be sticking out and getting bent as your bike is thrown into the hold. Wrap it up in a plastic bag along with the chain. Duct-tape it to the rear triangle, safely out of the way.

6 Bike boxes do protect bikes from impact, but I still place spacers in the rear dropouts and forks, just in case baggage handlers decide to run the box over... This type of chain hanger will keep the ends protected and prevent the chain from flapping around.

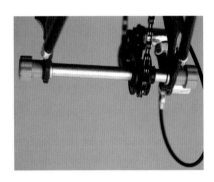

7 If you're packing your bike in a bike box, you may well have to remove the handlebars to fold the bike flat. Tighten the bolts that you've removed to prevent losing them, wrap the bars in bubble wrap, and duct-tape anything in place that could damage your paintwork and components in transit.

8 Use plenty of pipe lagging (insulating tubes) to protect the frame and forks. Wrap some around the forks and the cranks too, as it absorbs a lot of shock.

9 Use a fork-end protector (readily available from bike shops) to protect the ends from drops and prevent the forks from being pushed inwards.

10 Remove bottle cages too, as they can get bent or, even worse, damage fragile frame tubes in the process. Store the bottles in them to save space and prevent them from getting damaged.

TRAVEL TIPS

It can ruin your holiday if the airline sends your bike somewhere else, so I usually pack my helmet, saddle, shoes and pedals in my hand luggage so I can hire a bike when I get there instead. At least I'll have all my familiar contact points with me. Double-check the airline's weight restrictions and book your bike on the flight as early as possible – be aware that many airlines charge a flat fee for transporting bikes, whether they're in a bag or box. Don't carry any energy drinks or bars with you – buy them at the destination, as they're heavy and bulky to carry. There may also be security issues with taking such items on board. Write down all your measurements and take a tape measure with you so you can set up your bike quickly and accurately when you arrive. Lastly, don't forget to pack your pump, tools and, most importantly, a pedal spanner.

WASHING AND CARING FOR YOUR BIKE

To keep your bike running smoothly and ensure that the components will last, wash your bike at least once a week – especially in the winter. Washing your bike is a great way to get close to it and inspect every aspect of its workings. Water gets into all the sensitive parts of your bike, so it's best to wash your bike with care. Wear some wellies, rubber gloves and waterproof clothing, as you'll then be able to concentrate on the job properly.

Pressure (jet) washers are certainly quick, but generally not a good idea for cleaning your bike as they tend to blow water into sealed units such as the headsets, forks, hubs and bottom brackets. They also ruin your cables and blow all the lubricant off your chain. So, it's far better to hand-wash your bike with a sponge and brush – this way your bike will last longer and perform better.

You may see pro bike mechanics using jet washers when the weather is bad, as it saves time, but they'll always use an airline and pay particular attention to drying off parts that may have been filled with water.

Find a suitable area to clean your bike. Be aware that you'll need plenty of water and that the by-products from washing a bike can be quite messy. Therefore, a concrete area with a water supply and a drain is best. Always clean the floor with a stiff brush

TOOLS REQUIRED

- Water
- Bucket
- Brushes (large to toothbrush-size)
- Portable workstand
- Spray-on bikewash
- Sponge
- Strong degreaser (citrus ones are good) for drivetrain parts
- Chain-cleaning device (see right for more on chain cleaning)
- Sprocket cleaner (narrow brush to get between gaps)

when you've finished, as the degreasing fluids can make the floor very slippery.

1 Always clean the under-side of the saddle and the seat post first, so you can place the bike into the workstand before you wash the rest of your bike (most work-stand clamps hold the seat post), and also because it's best to start at the top of the bike and work down so you don't get muck on stuff you've already washed.

2 Once the bike is in the stand, drop both of the wheels out, as they're far easier to clean when they're out of the bike. Insert a chain roller to hold the chain in place. This will also help you clean the chain, let you rotate the chain and cranks easily, and keep the chain out of the way as you wash the rest of the bike.

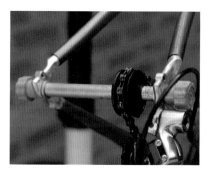

3 Use a spray-on de-greaser. You can dilute these cleaning sprays with water, as they tend to be quite concentrated and powerful. Be careful to read the instructions, as these fluids can be caustic and affect the finish of your bike. Most are not too kind to your hands either, so it's best to wear rubber gloves.

4 Brush the whole drive train with stronger degreaser solution. The citrus stuff is usually best for this. Work into the gear mechanisms and the chain rings, and leave it to penetrate for a few minutes.

5 Clean the chain with either a brush or with a chain-cleaning machine like this one. They can take the fuss out of getting the worst mess off the chain, but the best way is to use a small brush and a little patience.

6 The chain-cleaner also means you can clean the chain regularly, even without washing the whole bike, and re-lubricate on to a clean chain. This will prevent the build-up of grime and will lengthen the life of your gear components.

7 Use a big brush to clean the chainrings and cranks. You'll need to re-apply degreaser several times to remove all the road dirt and oil residue. Keep scrubbing until it has all gone.

8 Use a sponge and plenty of water to wash off any detergent and solvents from the drivetrain. Clean out the pedals and the shoe cleats using a smaller, toothbrush-size brush. Keep the pedal springs well lubricated and check their tension regularly.

9 Then you can start to clean the wheels. Clean the cassette first. Again, a strong degreaser is best, as it'll shift the greasy black stuff faster.

10 You can then clean and inspect the hubs too. Work into all the dirt with a longer brush and some mild degreaser, as you want to prevent it entering the freewheel mechanism but still shift all the gear debris.

11 Clean all the muck out of the sprockets with a suitable implement. There are such things as sprocket-cleaners, but you can just use a stiff brush. It's very important to keep the cassette clean, so it's sometimes worth removing it and giving it a thorough scrub.

12 A strip of fabric can also quickly clean all the goo from your gears. It'll also dry off the sprockets and clean the sides of the gear ramps, and prevent the rust from gathering.

13 Use a milder degreaser on the tyres and rims. Soak the rims and tyres, and leave for a moment before starting to scrub.

14 Once the road and brake dirt starts to lift, scrub the tyres and rims thoroughly with a stiff brush and lots of water. Once they're clean, rinse completely with clean water and dry off with a rag. Pay close attention to the rims and the bead area where muck can accumulate and assist in the breakdown of the brake pads.

15 Remove any debris from the slots in the brake pads and clean the brake mechanisms – use a pointed implement to push out any road grit and brake pad dust. Wash the brakes and pads with a sponge and be careful not to mis-align the calliper as you clean.

16 Be careful when cleaning the gear shifters and brake levers too – don't spray degreaser directly on the seals, and clean them with a rag rather than a stiff brush. Spraying water and degreaser into the internals will cause problems in the future.

17 Lubricate the chain with a suitable lube and use a light spray-lube on any gear and brake pivots (not the brake shoes or pads though!).

18 Rub away any lube residue from the chain with a clean cloth, and clean the jockey wheels in the rear mech, as these can spread dirt all around the clean drive train.

19 Lastly, give the paint a buff with some frame polish and a duster. Inspect the frame for damage and make sure that all the components are dry and free from degreaser residue.

PRO TIPS

1 Always work at a good height and use a solid workstand – it saves your back and means you'll take more care over the washing.

2 When it's wet always wash your bikes immediately, as once all the road dirt and grime is dry the bike is far harder to clean.

3 Keep the degreaser close to hand – here it's stored in an old water bottle held in the bottle cage – as this saves time and avoids waste.

04

WHEELS

Much as I love wheelbuilding, this is not the place to show you how to do it. Gerd Schraener's *The Art of Wheelbuilding* (Ann Arbor Press, 1999) and Jobst Brandt's *The Bicycle Wheel* (Avocet Inc, 1993) both offer excellent tuition and guidance in this very technical process. Wheelbuilding is involved rather than difficult and the fact that there are complete books written on the subject speaks for itself. So, first I'll just show you the basics of wheel truing, and hope you'll get the bug and want to learn more about how wheels are built.

TRUING WHEELS

Firstly, assess the wheel and decide where the imbalance could be. Spin the wheel and see where the buckles are and where the wheel has uneven tension. A wheel is like a suspension bridge, and any imbalance in the supports (spokes) places more stress on the neighbouring supports. The most common problem is a broken spoke, but spokes can also be loose or damaged, which will also cause a wobble.

When you spin the wheel, it should sit centrally in the jig (or bike if you're out riding). Your job is to find out where, and more importantly how, the wheel is being pulled away from this centre line. Don't attempt to true a wheel until you've a good idea what is causing the buckle.

Lateral (side-to-side) buckles are the easiest to solve:

- if the wheel hops to the left, tighten the spoke on the right or loosen the spoke on the left;

- if the wheel hops to the right, tighten the spoke on the left or loosen the spoke on the right.

However, radial (up-and-down) buckles are a little different:

- if the hop is towards the hub, the spoke is too tight;

- if the hop is away from the hub, the spoke is too loose.

TOOLS REQUIRED

- **Truing stand**
- **Spoke keys**
  (there are a variety of nipple sizes depending on spoke type and gauge)
- **Dishing stick**
- **Spoke tension meter (optional)**

So, if the rim hops to the left and towards the hub at the same time, there's a spoke pulling too tightly on the left, and if the rim hops to the right and away from the hub at the same time, there's a loose spoke on the right.

That's the simple version – the rest is about practice and experience, just like tuning a piano, apparently. The first few times you true a wheel will take you some time, but if you can be patient (and practise) it'll come as second nature. Remember to make small adjustments at first, and mark the rim with chalk or wrap a strip of tape on the suspect spokes so that you always know where you started.

Rear wheels have tighter spokes on the drive side than they do on the non-drive side. The non-drive spokes are also longer. This means that they require fewer turns than the drive side – it depends on the wheel, but the ratio is about 2:1. On front hubs you'll always need to loosen or tighten the same amount on both sides. Make sure you do it gradually and in no more than quarter- or half-turns at a time.

1 The usual cause of a buckle is a broken spoke (for more on replacing spokes, see pages 56-57) – however, here we are trying to find the loose ones that may just require tightening. Grab several spokes at a time and squeeze them to feel where the problem loose areas are before you start to true the wheel.

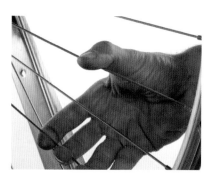

2 Always use a spoke key that fits the nipples snugly. A loose-fitting key will ruin the nipple very easily, especially if the nipple is tight. If the spoke becomes very tight and the rim still needs to move some more, you may have to loosen the opposite spoke to allow a little more movement. Spokes tighten with a standard right-hand thread, so if you're using your right hand you'll need to turn the spoke key towards you to tighten the spoke and away from you to loosen it.

3 A severe radial hop or a skip in the rim can signify a set or group of very loose or tight spokes. As with the lateral truing, you need careful judgment to decide which spokes to tackle first. Try to find the loose ones first. Then, using quarter-turns only, adjust the tension in two or four spokes at a time on each side (shown here with the red and black spoke keys) – you need to pull on both sides equally to prevent the wheel going out laterally as well as radially.

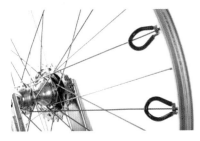

4 'Dish' describes the shape of the wheel. The hub lock nuts (where the wheel is held in the frame or forks) and the rim need to sit in line for the bike to handle properly. Wheel dish is determined by measuring the wheel with a dishing stick, which checks that the lock nuts are equally spaced on either side of the rim. Dish guarantees that the wheels will run in line and also allows for efficient braking.

5 Accurate truing has to be done using a quality wheel jig rather than with the wheel still in the bike. Wheel jigs provide more stability, so the wheel doesn't rock around when you spin it. The wheel jig pictured here has self-centring jaws and retaining arms so that the rim will be perfect if it's trued to the guides. The jaws can be adjusted so that the rim drags on them to give you a visual and audible clue as to where the buckle is.

6 Professional wheel builders will use a DT spoke tension meter. This can accurately measure spoke tension and enables a good wheelbuilder to keep variation in spoke tension to around 10 per cent. This is also useful when truing a wheel, as you can assess which spokes are being pushed too hard and are therefore likely to break first.

7 Once you're happy that the wheel is perfectly round again, carefully 'stress' it (twist it laterally in opposite directions) in your lap or gently on the floor. Don't stress the wheel with your full weight, especially if the bearings are sealed as they're vulnerable to side loads. You'll hear the wheel click and ping as the spokes 'find' their position. This may mean that the rim moves a little, so double-check it in the jig before you're finished.

8 Finally, replace the rim tape. I always use tape that will stick to the rim – this way you know it won't come loose and move around under the tube. Plastic tape is better than cloth, as cloth tape holds water and will rust the eyelets, which in turn can seize the nipples. Rim tape should be renewed every time rims are removed – never re-use old tape.

REPLACING SPOKES

Replacing a spoke is a straightforward operation, but it can be time-consuming. Spokes normally break as a wheel is reaching the end of its serviceable life, so it's worth considering a rebuild after you break one. Repeated spoke failure (where you've broken several spokes one after the other) usually means that the rim is wrecked and the spokes are struggling to support it. Properly built wheels from a good wheelbuilder won't break spokes, unless the spokes are damaged somehow, e.g. by repeated heavy impacts. Properly tensioned hand-built wheels are less likely to fail and are a wise investment.

Broken spokes usually occur on the drive side of the rear wheel. With track and single-gear wheels, broken spokes are less common, as there's less dish in the rear wheel and therefore the spokes are under less strain on the drive side. To replace a drive side spoke, you'll first have to remove the cassette sprockets (see page 116).

TOOLS REQUIRED

- **Spoke key**
- **Spare spokes (make sure you have the correct length)**
- **Screwdriver and/or**
- **Nipple-driver**
- **Truing stand**

1 If the head of the spoke faces into the hub centre (outbound), you'll have to thread the spoke in from the opposite side of the wheel. Spokes cross three times between the hub and the rim, either crossing under twice and over once, or over twice and under once. Either way, it's essential that you copy this lacing to maintain the integrity and strength of the wheel.

2 The spoke can pass through the lower part of the spokes on the opposite side of the wheel. However, lacing is trickier if the head of the spoke faces out from the hub centre (inbound). You have to angle the spoke upwards so that it avoids the crossing at the other side of the wheel. Be careful not to bend the spoke too much and weaken it.

3 In order to lace the spoke around the rim, you'll have to push it under the rim. Protect the rim from being scratched by the threads when you do this by placing a finger or thumb over the end of the spoke, at the same time bending the spoke very gently and evenly so that it can tuck under the rim.

RIM HEALTH

Most rims designed for use with rim brakes have a wear indicator, which is either a black line or a series of dots on the middle of the rim. As the rim wears, these marks very slowly disappear, and when you can't see them any more, the rim needs changing. It's very important to keep an eye on this, as the rims can wear severely and, combined with the pressure in the tyre, the bead on the rim will eventually fail. This can be catastrophic. The tube immediately explodes and the tyre is blown off the rim. The remaining part of the rim can easily tangle in the frame and, if it's the front wheel, you can have a very nasty accident. Don't risk setting off with old rims and wheels – strong wheels will save you a long walk home.

4 The correct-length spoke will meet the rim eyelet and should be long enough to pass through the nipple and be level with the top of it on the inside of the rim. Any longer and the spoke will be too slack on the nipple. The nipple can be replaced if necessary – nipples can round off with poorly fitting spoke keys, and poor-quality nipples can shear off.

5 Take up the slack with a screwdriver (or nipple-driver as shown here) before you start to true the wheel. Make a note of how far the other spokes protrude from the nipple and – if you have the correct-length spoke – you can get the spoke to a similar position. See pages 54-55 for more on truing wheels.

SPOKE TIPS

1   Always have another wheel handy so you can copy the spoke pattern, especially if you're replacing more than one spoke.

2   Use a nipple driver to run nipples on to the spoke threads. Stop when the nipple just reaches the end of the threaded section.

3   Carefully bed in the elbows of the spokes by using either your thumb or the face of a plastic mallet.

4   In emergencies, you can replace the spoke with the tyre in place, but only if you have exactly the right length of spoke. It's always best to remove the tyre, tube and rim tape so that you can access the nipple and replace it if necessary. Overlong spokes will protrude into the rim cavity and burst the tube, so make sure you take care when picking the replacement spoke.

5   Use brass washers (DT Swiss make these) on loose spoke holes. Some wheel builders 'set' the nipples into the holes with a nail punch – be careful when using bonded or lightweight hubs, though.

6   Adjust your rear mech (see pages 120-123) if the chain over-shifts from the lowest gears and into the spokes. This can damage the spokes, and cause them to break at a later date. Also, if the rear mech hits the spokes it can rip the gear mechanism off and/or ruin the wheel, so adjust it even if it makes the slightest noise.

7   Modern road bike wheelsets usually have a special type of spoke, most commonly with a straight head, rather than an elbow like a standard spoke. Always check with manufacturers and websites to see which one you'll need.

6 Eyeletted rims last longer than non-eyeletted ones and experience fewer breakages, as the eyelets allow the nipples to move slightly inside the rim. The eyelets also reinforce the rim and are easier to true, as the nipples move freely inside them.

SHIMANO AND CAMPAGNOLO ROAD HUBS

CUP-AND-CONE HUBS

Cup-and-cone hubs with loose bearings are very simple to service. The first few times it can be challenging, but experience really speeds the process up. The key is to make sure that all the components are in top condition – any wear and tear to the cones or bearings means that the parts should be replaced.

Most Shimano road hubs, from Tiagra to Dura Ace, use the same principle and many older Campagnolo hubs also follow the same pattern. Most contemporary Campagnolo hubs from Mirage to Record have an oversized aluminium axle and a system that requires no specialist cone spanners or tools – they have several specific parts but are simple to adjust, and everything is replaceable and serviceable.

HOW OFTEN SHOULD I STRIP THE HUBS?

Hubs will need a complete service every four to six months, depending on weather conditions and how often you ride. Fresh grease and regular adjustment will keep hubs rolling for a long time. Shimano cone hubs are excellent because you can rebuild

TOOLS REQUIRED

- **2 x 13mm cone spanners (Shimano use 13mm cones, but they can vary in size)**
- **Torque wrench**
- **17mm open-ended spanner (or cone spanner)**
- **Grease**
- **Axle vice and bench-mounted vice**
- **10mm Allen key**

them very easily and quickly, and they use top-quality bearings and hardened steel cones. Look after them properly and they'll easily outlast the spokes and the rims.

However, loose hubs don't last very long. Grab your wheel by the tyre and shake the wheel from side to side while it's still in the bike. If you feel a slight knock or 'play' through the tyre, the hub is loose. This means that the bearings are bashing around inside the hub and slowly disintegrating, and the seals are more exposed, allowing water and muck into the hub. Leave the hub like this and it won't take long for the internals to fail completely. Rebuilding the wheel with a new hub is far more costly and time-consuming than replacing the grease and the bearings every few months.

SHIMANO FRONT HUBS

1 The key to easy hub servicing is only working on one side. If you keep one side intact, the factory setting spacing over the lock nuts is easier to retain. All front hubs measure 100mm over the lock nuts – this measurement is critical so that the wheel can easily be replaced in the forks.

2 Undo and remove the lock nut, the washer and, finally, the cone. Cone spanners are very thin and flat. This means that they can fit into the machined flats on the sides of the cone and can adjust and tighten the cones without snagging on the washer and lock nut. Use the correct size (and don't use cone spanners to remove your pedals, as this will damage them!). Hold the cone with a cone spanner and release the lock nut with a 17mm spanner.

3 The cone is made from hardened steel and has a highly polished bearing surface. Inspect the cone carefully for any rough patches on the surface – this is known as pitting. On most front wheels there's only a cone, washer and lock nut.

4 Remove the cone, spacers and – very carefully – the axle. I find it's best to do this over something that will catch the bearings should they fall out – at least place your hand over the end. Place the threaded components down on the work-bench in the order they came off the hub to help you remember the order to return them in. Clean the axle and cones, leaving one side on the axle and in one piece.

5 Keep all the old bearings so that you can check you're replacing the same size and quantity. It's good practice to replace the bearings after every strip-down. The bearings are slightly more vulnerable than the cones and the hub surfaces, so they tend to wear out first. Look at them closely and you'll see tiny potholes. Bearings need to be mirror-finished, so if they're even slightly dull they need replacing. It's useful to have a magnetic screwdriver for this job, as it'll make re-installation far easier. Store spare bearings on a magnet to make them easier to manage.

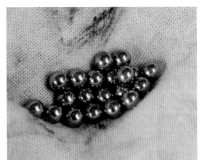

6 Clean the inside of the bearing surfaces and inspect for damage. If the bearing surfaces and cones are pitted, you'll need to replace either the cones or the hub assembly. Replacing the cones and the bearings, and resetting them in grease, will usually solve any hub roughness.

7 To grease the hub cups properly, you don't have to remove the hub seals – they're factory fitted and are very hard to replace properly, as they're pressed into the shell of the hub, and it's possible to see into the hub with the seals in place. However, if you do have to remove them, be very careful. Wrap a rag around a tyre lever and prise the seals out carefully. Don't use a screwdriver as this can bend the seal, and if that happens you'll never get it back in again. To replace the seal, use your fingers to locate it and then tap it home using a rubber mallet.

8 When all the bearings are installed, take the loose cone and push it back into the hub. Rotate it a couple of times to seat the bearings. This will also tell you if there's any damage to the bearing surface inside the hub, and will stick the bearings in place so you can turn the wheel over

to do the other side. Next, double-check that there are the right amount of bearings in the hub. Lastly, smear a little more grease on top of the bearings and check there isn't any grease inside the hub. You'll then be able to push the axle through without making a big mess.

9 Replace the axle (remember to return it the same way round as it was at removal). As you've only disturbed one set of bearings, the spacing won't have been altered. Screw the cone onto the axle and up to the bearings.

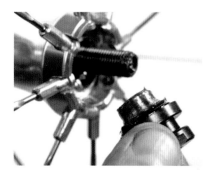

10 Spin the axle in your fingers and 'rock' it slightly from side to side – you're looking for the point at which there's no 'play', only smooth spinning. When you're happy that the bearings are running smoothly, replace the washer and then the lock nut. At this stage they need to be finger-tight.

11 With practice, you'll be able to set the cones like this and simply do up the cone as in step 2. However, when you tighten the lock nut for the last time, you may also either loosen the cone slightly or tighten it. Most hubs have seals in the hub body that will drag a little when the cone is set. To set the cones properly you'll need two cone spanners (13mm for front hubs) – with two spanners you can work the cones against each other. So, if you over-tighten the lock nut, place the two cone spanners on either side of the hub and slightly undo the cones until the axle spins freely.

HUB CHECK

Replace the wheel into the bike and check for play by rocking the wheel from side to side. Then pick up the bike and spin the wheel quickly. Hold on to either fork leg. You may feel a rumbling of vibration through the fork, in which case the cones are too tight. Re-check the cones again after your first ride. Using an axle vice to hold the wheel steady will help if your hub isn't built into a wheel, but isn't necessary if the wheel is complete.

Axle vices are made from a soft material and clamp the axle tightly so you can work on the hub with both hands, which will speed things up. The best way to work on a hub as a part of the wheel is on top of a workbench with the hub at a slight angle so you can see into the internals.

SHIMANO REAR HUBS

Much of the information in the front hub section (see previous pages) applies to rear hubs too. The process is the same, even though the unit is bigger and there's a drive mechanism involved too. Rear hub spacing is usually 130mm across the lock nuts.

Most of these freewheel cassette bodies can be replaced, which can prolong the hub's life indefinitely. If both cones need to be replaced, it's worth measuring the position of the lock nut and cones before you start work. Measure the distance from the end of the axle to the side of the first lock nut. Then, when you start to remove the cones, work on one side at a time and place the components down in the order that they're removed. I thread them over a screwdriver or an Allen key in reverse order, which makes replacement easy.

Cones are a specific size and you must use the correct part, otherwise the hub won't work properly. So if you have to replace anything, check that you're using the right part number for that particular hub. This also applies to cassette bodies, as there are different sizes for eight- and nine-/ ten-speed, and Dura Ace cassette bodies are of a better quality too.

TOOLS REQUIRED

- **Cone spanners (the Shimano rear hub has 15mm cones, but they do vary in size)**
- **17mm open-ended spanner (or cone spanner)**
- **10mm Allen key**
- **Grease**
- **Axle vice and bench-mounted vice**
- **Cassette service and replacement tools**
- **Chain whip**
- **Cassette lock ring tool and spanner/wrench**
- **Torque wrench**

1 Remove the cassette using a chain whip and a cassette-removing tool (see page 116 for how to do this). This will allow you to access the cones that are obscured by the cassette sprockets and lockring.

2 Flip the hub over and work on the non-drive side. Hold the cone with a cone spanner and undo the lock nut. Leave the drive side intact to ensure that the spacing remains identical – this is especially important with the rear hub, as uneven spacing can affect the chainline and the gear shifting.

3 Remove the axle from the drive side, clean the parts and check the cones for signs of wear, especially pitting.

4 Be careful to collect all the bearings – sometimes these will need to be fished out with a suitable screwdriver. As with the front hubs, set all the axle components to one side and clean the hub bearing surfaces.

5 Once the hub is cleaned, you can remove the cassette body with a 10mm Allen key. The cassette body is usually factory fitted and tight, so you'll need an appropriate Allen key (i.e. a long one). You may need to use a pipe for a little extra leverage to undo the bolt.

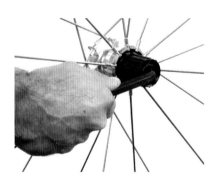

6 Only remove the cassette body if it requires replacing. Here you can see that the cassette body is located on a spline on the side of the hub.

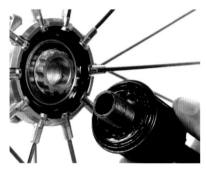

7 The bolt that retains the cassette body can be fully removed and the cassette body can be replaced if necessary. Be careful not to lose the washer that sits on the inside of the body. Set the torque wrench to 34.3-49Nm and re-tighten the bolt.

8 Grease and reset the bearings into the hub. 9×1/4in bearings are usually required, but, as with the front hub, double-check that you're returning the same amount as you removed. It's impossible to detect damage to the surface of the bearings, so new ones must be used to ensure smooth running. Take your time and set the bearings in grease so that they're covered and the grease is worked in.

9 The grease will be enough to hold the bearings in place, but carefully re-insert the axle, with the drive-side spacers and cones still in place, from the drive side. It is best to do this over the bench incase the bearings decide to escape.

10 If you've disturbed the drive side cones or replaced them, you'll have to accurately set and tighten the drive side before reassembling the hub, as once the axle is in place it's difficult to access the cones on the drive side.

11 Once the axle is complete, you can return it to the hub. Spin the non-drive side cone onto the axle and set the cone finger-tight. Check that the axle rotates easily and there's no drag or notchy feeling to the axle. Add any spacers, washers and finally the lock nut.

12 Then set the cones. This is harder with the rear hub because the drive-side cone is tucked into the cassette body. It's therefore far easier to do this job with the wheel secured in an axle vice, and some mechanics even adjust the hub when it's back in the bike. However, this requires experience.

GREASE

Every mechanic has a favourite hub grease. The secret is to use a specially formulated synthetic bicycle grease that's waterproof and of a consistent quality, but also not to overdo it, as this can make the bearings drag and adjustment more difficult. Many of the non-synthetic or engineering-type greases are too heavy for hub bearings. Also, avoid lithium (usually white-coloured) grease, as it's easily washed out of the bearings and breaks down after repeated revolutions. Shimano hub grease is excellent, as is Finish Line, Park, Pedros and Rock 'n' Roll. Use a grease gun with a fine nozzle to direct grease where you want it – this will avoid waste.

CAMPAGNOLO HUBS

FRONT HUB

The axle is aluminium and is very strong. Only one end of the axle unscrews, and the cones are held in place with a collar that can easily be adjusted to take up any play in the hub.

1 Undo the axle end bolt with two 5mm Allen keys (see step 1 of rear hub servicing opposite) and remove the end – this is the part that retains the wheel in the forks and also allows the QR levers to fit through the hub.

2 Undo the retaining screw on the collar adjustment (this is either a cross-headed screw or a 3mm Allen screw).

3 Remove the adjustment collar, which threads to the outside of the axle – once this is removed, the axle is free, although the cone may still be held tight to the axle next to the bearings. A very gentle tap with a plastic mallet may be required to shift it.

4 Now pull the axle out. The bearings are held in plastic clips and under the white weather seals. The weather seals are very delicate, so it's best to leave them in place and work around them.

5 Strip out the bearings and replace if necessary. Flush out all the dirt and old grease with degreaser and make sure that the insides are clean and dried with a rag. Grease both sets of bearings before reassembling the axle with good-quality waterproof grease.

6 Replace the axle with the cone collar on the fixed side. The adjustable side cone slips over the axle and rests on the bearings. Check the cone for pitting and replace the cone if necessary.

7 There's a split washer/spacer that centres the axle over the cone. Once this is in place, the threaded collar can be replaced and the cones set without any play – this is usually done to finger-tightness.

8 The fixed side of the hub has a dust cover that snaps into place over the axle and keeps the weather and muck out. Replace the QR and you're ready to ride. If the hub still has play in it when it's back in the forks, remove and retighten the adjustable collar.

REAR HUB

See page 116 for the full details on removing cassettes, as you'll need to do this before servicing the hubs.

1 Undo the end cap with two 5mm Allen keys – this will unscrew the axle end of the non-drive side.

2 Remove the end cap on the non-drive side and the thin washer just behind it.

3 You can then undo and remove the adjusting collar from the axle. On this Record hub the retaining bolt requires a 3mm Allen key.

4 The collar may be tight, although it can usually be removed with your fingers. This also demonstrates how to adjust the play out of the hubs when rebuilding them, with a spanner on the adjustment collar and an Allen key in the end of the axle.

5 As with the front hub you'll now see a split washer and the weather seals, but unlike the front hub the axle won't be free just yet.

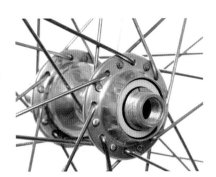

6 Turn the wheel around and use a 17mm cone spanner to undo the cassette-body locking collar. This is a left-hand thread (anti-clockwise) and the axle needs to be trapped at the same time with a 5mm Allen key in the fixed, drive-side axle end.

7 There's a direction arrow marked on the cassette-body locking collar. Remove the collar from the axle end.

8 The cassette body will now easily pull away from the hub. Thoroughly clean and degrease the pawls and internals of the ratchet ring on the hub body. Rebuild using a very light grease and use it sparingly as too much can cause the pawls to drag.

9 The internals are as on a sealed bearing hub body (see page 70), although Campagnolo pawls are retained in a circular spring clip, which prevents them from falling out when you pull the cassette body away. You can use an old toothbrush to get the freewheel mechanism really clean.

10 Check and grease the main axle bearings in both the drive and non-drive side of the hub shell – as with the front hub, don't attempt to remove the white weather seals.

11 The cone slides onto the axle, which can then be re-installed into the hub body. When the axle is pushed back into the hub, the cone collar will seat into the bearings. Turn the axle in the bearings and check for any 'notchy' feeling, which may denote worn bearings or pitted cones.

12 Turn the wheel over and reinstate the non-drive side cone collar – as with the front hub this simply slides over the axle and into place.

13 Refit the split retaining washer and the adjusting collar (as on the front hub). Now adjust the bearings and nip up. Before replacing the cassette body, check the hub for play and re-adjust until the bearings feel silky smooth.

14 Once the axle is reinstated, and you're happy that the bearings are properly serviced, turn the wheel over and replace the cassette body – the pawls may require some fiddling to get into position, but the system is pretty simple. Replace the cassette-body locking collar (tightens anti-clockwise) and lastly the non-drive side axle end.

CARTRIDGE BEARING HUBS

The following method for fitting new bearings in hubs with cartridge units is fairly straightforward. Each manufacturer will have its own tools and bearings, but the principles remain very similar. Cartridge bearing hubs rely on a sealed-bearing cartridge unit that can be removed and replaced, whereas cup-and-cone systems rely on loose ball bearings and adjustable bearing surfaces.

The ball bearings are set into a hardened steel cartridge casing that press-fits into the hub shell or freewheel body. This unit is packed with grease and sealed with plastic or labyrinth seals. The quality is determined by the number of bearings and amount of grease packed into them.

Once the bearing is pushed into the hub, the axle is then press-fitted into the hole through the middle of the cartridge. All this has to be a precise and tight fit to support the wheel and to spin efficiently. This gives you a smooth spinning feel, as there's less chance of over-tightening the bearing with lock nuts and cones.

The obvious advantage of sealed cartridge bearings like this is that they require less adjustment and servicing than standard cup-and-cone bearings. However, they're only as good as the quality of the bearings and standard of engineering of the hub shells. A cartridge hub at the cheaper end of the range may have push-fit covers and less sealing than a Shimano or Campagnolo cup-and-cone hub. So, shop wisely, as good-quality hubs can be built several times over into fresh rims, and last much longer than cheap ones.

Sealed bearings don't like side loads and can easily be damaged, so always use the manufacturer's recommended tools to remove them.

1 The spacers at the end of each side of the axle are either push-fitted or locked into place with a threaded lock ring. Sometimes a grub screw can lock them in place. The ones shown here require an Allen key and a cone spanner to undo the cassette-retaining spacer.

2 This non-drive-side spacer threads onto the axle end – most are a simple push-on fitting. The axle and the bearing take the strain, so oversize axles are a good idea with sealed bearings, as they fit better, can handle much more abuse and tend to

twist less under drive. Power transfer to the rear wheel should be better and the bearings should last longer.

3 With the spacers and lock nuts removed, the cassette body can be taken off. On most cartridge hubs the cassette will be a push fit secured by the drive-side spacer. However, some use a Shimano-type cassette freewheel body that's bolted to the hub body. You'll need a 10mm Allen key to remove this.

4 Push out the old cartridge bearings. This wheel's axle has to be tapped out with a plastic mallet. Once one side has been removed, the cartridge will pop out, still attached to the axle. The axle can then be used to tap out any bearings remaining in the hub shell.

5 This Bontrager hub has a bolt-on cassette body and is removed in the same way as a Shimano hub (see step 3) with a 10mm Allen key. You can see the collar that holds the cartridge bearing. This needs to be cleaned thoroughly before a new bearing can be installed.

6 The remaining bearing on the axle can be tapped off by placing the axle in a die. This allows you to use the axle as a drift to remove the remaining bearing on the other side of the hub. To replace the bearing you'll have to place it on top of the die and tap the axle back in. When it's flush to the shoulder in the centre of the axle, it's ready to be reinstalled on the hub.

7 The new bearings can be replaced. All sealed bearings have a code number and can be bought at most engineering suppliers or your local bike shop.

8 Use an appropriate die to seat the new bearings into the hub. They're a tight fit, but must be installed gently so as not to damage the bearing unit or the seals. Put some grease around the outside of the bearing and place it squarely onto the hub. Use an insertion tool that's the same size as the outer metal part of the bearing. Any side load onto the black plastic seal part of the bearing will ruin it. Gently tap the bearing home with the plastic mallet.

SEALED BEARINGS

- Remove sealed bearings with an old axle or soft drift. Be careful not to damage the inside of the hub body – a light tap should be enough to free the cartridges.

- With care, the seals can be removed with a scalpel blade and the old grease flushed out with degreaser. Use a grease gun to inject fresh grease into the bearings inside the collars.

- Avoid strong solvent-based lubricants on sealed bearing hubs, as they can damage the seals and flush out the grease from the bearings.

9 Most cartridge bearing hubs have their own type of cassette. They usually pull off once the lock rings and spacers have been removed. Inside the hub is a series of teeth and on the cassette body are three sprung pawls. These pawls engage with the teeth when you pedal and 'click' around freely when you stop pedalling. The hub pictured here has one circular spring that holds the pawls in place.

10 Here you can see the serrated part inside the hub. This needs to be completely cleaned out and lightly greased before you replace the rebuilt cassette body.

11 Carefully remove the pawls and clean all the dirty grease off the cassette body. Use a toothbrush to clean out all the pawl indentations and spring channels.

12 The cassette shown here has a single circular spring, so the pawls need to be set in grease and then have the spring replaced over them. This does take time, as it's quite fiddly. Many hubs have springs for individual pawls. If these fail they'll need replacing, as they can get stuck into the serrated parts and ruin the freewheel.

13 Use a lightweight grease on the freewheel pawls to avoid chain sag. To replace the cassette body and fit it into the hub, you'll need to push the pawls into the body. Some hubs supply a ring clip tool for this – a cotton thread can also be wrapped around them and removed as the body pushes home. Once placed, double-check that the cassette body rotates freely before you rebuild the rest of the hub.

MAVIC WHEELS

Mavic hubs have used sealed bearings for over 30 years, and they make excellent units. I've featured them here because they're very popular and use the same hub arrangement for most of their wheelsets, and pretty much the same design across their range. Regular servicing of the freewheel and cassette body is recommended – at least twice a year – usually when replacing cassette sprockets.

Thorough degreasing and rebuilding will keep the freewheel running smoothly and prevent wear to the mechanism. The design is pretty simple but very efficient, so Mavic hubs are very easy to service without specialist tools – and because they're popular, spares and replacement bearings can be easily sourced and replaced.

FRONT WHEELS

1 The end caps are a push fit onto the ends of the axle. They should pull off pretty easily, and are held in place with a notch machined into the axle and a rubber ring on the inside of the end cap.

2 The plastic Mavic peg tool (supplied with the wheels) is all you need to remove the collar that retains the axle and seals out the dirt.

3 The axle has a 5mm Allen socket machined into it so that you can capture the axle and prevent it from rotating. A few turns will loosen the collar easily.

4 With the collar removed, the axle should now be loose in the hub. It's rare that this seizes into the cartridges – if it has, a gentle tap with a plastic mallet should do the trick.

5 Pull out the aluminium axle – this will expose the bearings and the hub shell.

6 This shows that there's only one threaded end, and this needs to be carefully cleaned, as it has a fine pitch thread for micro-adjusting the bearing drag when the wheel is reassembled.

7 Remove the old cartridge bearings and press in new ones (see cartridge hub servicing on pages 70-71), then rebuild the hub. Use light grease on the axle bearing surfaces and replace the dust cover and end caps.

8 The bearings can be adjusted for drag once the wheel has been replaced into the forks. Simply spin the wheel, and tighten or loosen the hub until it spins freely and without any play. Check the wheels regularly and spin the axles in your fingers to feel for notchy or seized bearings.

REAR WHEELS

1 Remove the cassette body and clean (see page 116). Disassembly starts on the non-drive side. The end caps push fit into the axle ends, so remove these first.

2 As with the front hub, you need to use the special Mavic tool to remove the dust collar – this also retains the axle.

3 Trap the axle with a 5mm Allen key and undo the collar on the non-drive side.

4 With the 5mm Allen key still in place, use a 10mm Allen key in the end of the axle on the non-drive side to undo the main axle from the cassette bolt on the drive side.

5 The non-drive-side portion of the axle will now slide out. This is oversized and provides added strength and stiffness to the rear wheel. The cartridge bearing on the non-drive side will need to be tapped out from the other side with a suitable drift.

6 The remaining stub of axle on the drive side can be removed from the cassette, and the cassette body will now be free to slide off the hub body.

7 The cassette body can now be cleaned and replaced. If there's a washer on the fixing bolt inside the cassette body and the hub, make sure that this is replaced when you rebuild so the cassette spins properly. Failure to do so will mean that the hub won't freewheel.

8 The bearings and the pawls for the freewheel remain on the hub body. Clean these with a degreaser and a tooth-brush. The bearings can also be replaced if necessary and the pawls and seals on the hub lubricated with a lightweight oil.

9 Once the hub is rebuilt and returned to the bike, the drag can be adjusted in the same way as the front wheel, with the wheel in the frame. Check for play and make sure that the QR lever is tight.

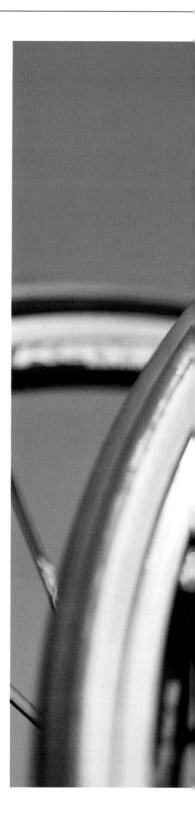

TYRES

SIZE

Like most theories, no one can decide on a trade-compatible system for measuring the width of cycle tyres. Tyre size is not normally the width across the treads, as you would think, but is based more on the size of the casings. Some have higher profiles and others have more rubber on the tread, which makes them appear larger. The European Tyre and Rim Technical Organisation (ETRTO) and the International Standards Organisation (ISO) use the same method to determine tyre width: take the distance between the two beads, measured over the tyre tread, and divide it by 2.5.

700c is now the internationally recognised tyre size for road bikes. 27in×1in or 27in×1 1/4in was once the 'British' size, but bikes have now standardised with the European measurement. This is the same measurement for tubular tyres, although they have a totally different rim (see page 86 for more on tubulars).

However, some manufacturers take the measurement on the casing side from the edge of the bead to the centre of the casing – thus some of their tyres can look large, as they use the same casing volume but larger treads.

TUBULAR v CLINCHER

The current trends for carbon rims and deep-section wheels mean that tubular tyres are having a bit of a renaissance – this is mainly because complicated rim shapes are hard to make from carbon,

although rim-makers are getting better and better at making clincher rims. See more on tubular tyres on page 86. A tubeless road system (like UST mountain bike wheels) is still in development. It does take a little more preparation time than a standard wheel, but the result is good and there's less chance of pinch flats and other inner tube problems. Clincher/tubulars are also available – these are tubular in construction but have a bead that locks into the standard-type clincher rim.

BEADING

All clincher tyres have a bead that runs around the edge of the tyre and secures the tyre by locking under the lip of the rim. Steel beads keep a circular shape and Kevlar beads are flexible, but both have similar strength. Steel-beaded tyres are slightly flexible so they stretch onto the rim – Kevlar doesn't stretch, so the beads are made a bit longer, which helps, but can make the procedure a bit of a handful. The main advantage with Kevlar is the weight you can save, and you can carry folded spares for longer trips. The main disadvantage is the price – Kevlar is an advanced material and costs much more.

COMPOUNDS

Different-coloured tyres often denote different hardness of the rubber compound. Some riders find softer rubber means much better grip on wet surfaces. Generally speaking, black tyres are harder than these and tend to last longer, but the quality of rubber can have a big effect on the amount of grip, and wear rate of your tyres. This is often reflected in the price too.

Softer and lighter racing tyres are more susceptible to flats and tend to wear more quickly. There's always a trade-off when trying to improve grip and lighten weight.

Assess the variables and choose a tread for its ride quality and value rather than its 'pose' appeal. Road conditions also play a major part in tyre choice. Northern European weather is incredibly tough on tyres.

FAT OR THIN?

Tread patterns are also affected by the section of the tyre – a tyre's width and height can alter your bike's handling characteristics just as much as the tread itself (if any). Fatter tyres give a bit more suspension to the ride, but also provide a larger surface area for drag, punctures, etc, while thinner tyres will transfer more shock through to your hands. As a rule, heavier riders prefer the fatter tyre option, but lighter people won't need so much cushioning from the ravages of the road surface.

The main road tyre sizes are 700×19c, 700×20c, 700×23c, 700×25c and 700×28c.

Wider tyres are available but are usually used on touring and commuter bikes. The narrower tyres tend to be used for track and time trial riding, while the fatter tyres are better for rough roads and training bikes. For most rides, a 700×23c tyre is ideal for all-round road surfaces.

Opinions vary on rolling resistance, tyre-width and the influence tyres have on aerodynamics, and much research has been done. A narrow tyre may appear to have less rolling resistance but this is not necessarily the case. I shan't enter into the debate here, but the quality of the rubber, the road surface and the tyre pressure play a major part, and width adds comfort and allows for better cornering grip – for longer rides this can only be a good thing. So my advice is to worry about comfort and ride quality before you start to consider weight and profiles. The key is to find the size that suits the riding you're doing and try to see the tyre inflated on a wheel before you buy.

PRESSURE

Tyre pressure can have a major effect on the handling and stability of your bike. Too much air gives you a quicker ride, but this is at the expense of comfort and might affect cornering grip. Too little air gives a squashy, sluggish but comfortable ride, but you may pick up thorns and can 'snakebite' (see below), puncturing the tyre more easily.

Look at the recommended pressures on the sidewall of the tyre and stick within the limits. Experiment with different conditions and pressures – try harder, narrower tyres for quick conditions and muddy roads, and softer, wider tyres for technical conditions or when you need more grip. As a rule, run your tyres five to ten per cent softer in the wet for extra grip.

DIRECTIONAL PROBLEMS

There are two types of directional tyres, front- or rear-specific, and dual purpose (the same tread for front and rear use). Directional tyres usually have a rotation arrow on the sidewall. If no arrows are apparent, the rule of thumb is to fit them with the arrow patterns pointing forwards in the direction of rotation.

GASHES AND SPLITS

Serious gashes in tyres often mean that the tube will push through it and burst. Emergency repairs can be done to save a long walk home or keep a tyre going for a little bit longer. See page 83 for more on repairing gashes.

Sidewall splits are a hazard of lightweight racing tyres. All-black tyres offer more sidewall protection as the rubber usually covers the whole tyre. Make sure your brake blocks are adjusted correctly, as they can cause some serious damage to the sidewalls.

TOP TYRE TIPS

1   Swap the front tyre with the back tyre on a regular basis. This will help your tyres last longer, as the rear tyre wears faster than the front.

2   New tyres can have a residue on them that can make them a bit slippery. A (careful) wet ride and a proper wash with degreaser will remove this pretty quickly.

3   Place a new inner tube in a plastic bag with a sprinkling of talc and give it a shake – this will coat the tube and help it slip into place under the tyre.

4   Check the treads regularly for flints and shards of glass. These will work their way through the tread and may puncture the tube several days after first being picked up. To remove these, let the tyre down first (as you could force the object in further by mistake) and use a sharp pointed implement to remove it.

SNAKEBITE PUNCTURES

Snakebite punctures occur when you've smacked something pretty hard (usually a stone, kerb or a pothole) and the tube is pinched between the object and the rim, making two holes on either rim edge – hence 'snakebite', as it looks like two teeth have punctured your tube. For more on how to repair these, see step 4 on page 82.

REMOVING TYRES AND REPLACING A TUBE

1 Fix good rim tapes to the wheel. Use tapes that stick to the rim base, as they're less likely to move when you inflate the tyre. Make sure that there are no sharp objects in the rim and that all the spoke holes are covered.

4 Slightly inflate the replacement tube with two strokes of a mini-pump, just enough for the tube to take shape but not so much that it becomes bigger than the diameter of the wheel. Next, insert the valve into the valve hole. Make sure that the valve is seated properly into the rim, then push the tyre over the top of the tube.

2 Most road tyres will come off easily with just one tyre lever. Push the tyre away to reveal the bead, slip the lever tip under the bead and simply pull the bead off. If you have to use two levers, pull one section off first and then move a little further around the rim. The second lever will be harder to pull, but should pop the tyre off easily. Run the lever around the rim, which will remove one side of the tyre from the rim. Don't remove the tyre completely at this point.

3 Pull the tube away from the tyre and pack it away – you can fix it later. Check that there's nothing wrong with the rim tape beneath the tube, as it can sometimes come loose under the tyre and move, exposing a spoke hole that can pinch the tube. Double-check the tyre walls for thorns and anything that may have penetrated the tyre. Be careful not to get any debris in there either, as it may be sharp and cause another flat on inflation.

5 Work the tube carefully into the carcass of the tyre, away from the rim, inflating it slightly more if necessary. Beware of folds in the tube at this point and don't twist the tube as you return it to the tyre – this can pinch and even puncture once re-inflated, and may also mean that the tyre will inflate unevenly.

6 Now, start to return the open side of the tyre bead into the rim. Start at the valve hole and work the tyre either side with two hands, until there's only a small amount left.

7 Pull the last part of the tyre onto the rim by hand, as a tyre lever can pinch the tube as you lever the tyre on. It can be a bit tricky with some tyres, so ask someone to help if possible. Once done, check that the bead hasn't snagged the tube or pinched it between the bead and the rim. This can push the tyre off the rim or make it roll unevenly, or even explode once the tyre has been pumped up to a decent pressure.

8 Finally, pump the tyre up to the recommended pressure. If the tyre doesn't run true (it wobbles as you spin the wheel), re-seat it by letting most of the air out and pulling the tyre away from the bead. This will help the bead sit into the rim and usually 'pops' the tyre into place. See over for more on mini-pumps.

MENDING A PUNCTURE ON THE ROAD

Punctures are a fact of cycling life, no matter how hard you try to avoid them. I have about 20-odd punctures every year, so mending them is far cheaper than using a new tube every time. If you ride through the autumn, when the hedges are clipped and there are more thorns on the road, or in the wet when flints and sharp grit are washed into the roads, you can expect several punctures.

Prevention can only be aided by running your tyres at their recommended pressures and replacing them regularly. Replacing a tyre can be done quickly with practice, but it's worth taking your time if you can, as you'll be less likely to make a mistake and risk flatting another tube. Also, try to get the tyre re-inflated as close as you can to the recommended pressure – even if your mini-pump takes forever, it'll help prevent another flat.

As soon as you realise you have a flat, stop. It's better to get on with fixing the flat than trying to ride any further on a potentially hazardous wheel. Riding with a flat can also damage the rim should you hit anything hard on the road. Stopping straight away may also allow you to find the hole in the tyre and remove any sharp objects that may have become trapped in the tread.

Remove the wheel and hang your bike up on a suitable hedge or tree branch. If the puncture is in the rear wheel, try not to dangle the chain on the ground. (See page 40 for more on removing wheels.)

Many riders carry at least two spare tubes all the time, and it's far better to replace the tube than try to patch it if you're out on the road. Who wants to wait for the glue to go off, try to keep the patches dry and try to sand some French chalk if it's snowing? Fixing tubes is best done in the dry, as it can take around ten minutes to mend each hole. If you use a decent puncture kit, it's highly unlikely that the patch will leak – in fact, Rema feathered-edge patches are actually stronger than the tube itself.

However, if you're out on the road or on a club run, it's far better to have several spare tubes with you so you can get back on your bike quickly and not hold anyone up.

VALVE TYPES

Presta (thin-type) or Schraeder (car-type) valves both have their benefits. Presta valves can handle greater pressures and don't leak as much as Schraeder valves. Presta valves are sealed by tightening the knurled nut at the end of the valve – to pump up the tyre, this must be undone.

However, Schraeder valves are easier to pump up and you can always top them up at a petrol station (though you must do this with extreme caution to avoid the tube exploding). The core can be replaced in most Schraeder valves and some Presta valves if they're leaking. Some tourists use Schraeder, but most road bikes will have Presta valves as standard.

'GLUELESS' PATCHES

Although not as permanent as the glue-and-patch variety, glueless patches can provide an emergency fix and work especially well if you're in a rush or if it's raining, as you don't have to wait for the glue to dry. As with standard patches, sand the area properly to help the patch fix to the tube. Then carefully peel a patch off its backing paper, place it over the hole and apply pressure with your thumb. The tube will be ready to re-install and inflate immediately.

PATCHING A PUNCTURE AND USING A MINI-PUMP

1 Find the hole. This is usually a case of pumping up the tube and listening. A bucket of water is not required for this – just keep pumping until you can hear the 'psssssss'. Once you have the hole, place your finger and thumb over it, as you don't want to lose it.

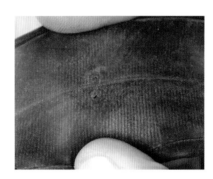

2 Rough up the area around the hole with some sandpaper. This will help the glue penetrate the rubber and ensure the patch adheres properly. The glue is a contact adhesive (it works when the patch is placed on it), but needs to be applied to a grease-free and dry tube in order to work properly.

3 Apply plenty of glue to the area, starting at the hole and working outwards. Keep an eye on where the hole is so you can get the patch over it properly later on. Leave the glue for five minutes until it's almost completely dry.

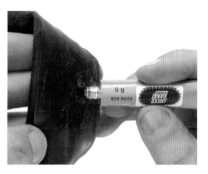

4 Most fixable holes are covered by a 2cm patch. Apply firm pressure to the patch with your thumb, as you want the patch to be fully in place before you re-inflate. Stretch the tube gently by pulling either side of the patch – this will show if it has stuck. If it's a 'pinch' flat or snakebite puncture, use two patches (one over each hole), rather than one big one.

5 Remove the plastic backing film from the centre. Don't pull it off from a corner, as it can pull the patch off with it. The backing is used to make sure you don't touch the underside of the patch, and so you can press it onto the tube easily.

6 If you can dust the area with French chalk or talc, this will prevent the glue from sticking to the inside of the tyre carcass and help it slide into place as you inflate the tyre.

RATTLING VALVES?

This is especially a problem with deep-section rims. Use some plumber's tape and wrap the valve with it before you install the tube.

7 Undo the small locking tip of the valve (Presta type only). Free it up by pressing it in a couple of times – this will enable the valve to pass air in easily, as it sometimes gets 'stuck' after full inflation.

8 Push the pump head firmly onto the valve. Sometimes you'll have to place a thumb behind the tyre to prevent the valve vanishing into the hole as you push it home (some valves have lock rings to prevent this).

9 All good mini-pumps have a locking lever. This ensures that the pump head makes an airtight seal over the valve and means you can concentrate on inflating the tyre. The valve internals

TYRE BOOT

Large tyre gashes need to be repaired because the tube will blister out of any holes in the tyre carcass and explode again. Tyre boots are best, but there are other emergency measures you can take if you're on the road. You can put a piece of cardboard, a used gel wrapper or a spare patch behind the gash – duct tape is also really sticky and strong, and gives added protection to the tube. Wrap a length around your mini-pump for such emergencies. Once the gash has been patched, pump up to a lower-than-normal pressure so as not to stress the damaged area, and ride carefully home.

can be removed and replaced as they wear out. The seal can also be swapped around to cope with either valve type (see your pump instructions, as this depends on the make).

10 Pump firmly, but don't rush. If you push too hard or at an awkward angle, you can bend the valve or snap the locking part off. Use all of the pump stroke and take your time. Pump the tyre up to the recommended pressure (or as close as you can).

TUBULAR TYRES

Whatever is said of the quality of high pressure (or clincher) bicycle race tyres, you still can't beat the rolling qualities of a tubular tyre ('tub' or 'sew-up'), mounted on to a set of lightweight 'sprint'-rimmed racing wheels.

Why? Well, for starters the rim is a far less complicated shape than its hooked-rimmed counterpart and compresses slightly under force so they are therefore more comfortable than clincher tyres at higher pressures. They can also be inflated up to 200psi and still retain their integrity, as the tube is stitched and encased in the tyre's carcass – clinchers would blow off the rim at anything over 150psi and would probably distort pretty soon after 130psi anyway.

The recent trend of deep-section and lightweight carbon rims has meant that the tubular tyre is having its very own renaissance, mainly down to the fact that it's very hard to make a good-quality carbon clincher rim, but also that the professional riders always ride tubular tyres – because they are arguably faster, more comfortable and much grippier in the wet. They also have the added advantage of not slipping off in the event of a puncture, so riders can still control

the bike in the event of a sudden flat (an essential feature if riding on the track).

Greg LeMond famously won the World Road Race championships on a 'soft' tub, something that would have been impossible on a clincher tyre.

A clincher tyre rolls dangerously when it is soft and can roll off the rim completely, which may mean a nasty fall and ruining your rims. Tubulars also rarely pinch-puncture, as they have no rim edge to get caught against and the tube cannot get snagged on spoke holes like its clincher counterpart, with it being protected and encased by the tyre's carcass.

Contrary to popular belief, tubulars are actually quite easy to install – it can be a bit messy the first few times you attempt it, but in time you get better at the job. Here's one way of sticking tubulars (once again every mechanic will have their preferred way of doing this). A strong firm grip is essential.

Before you start, practise the mounting procedure a couple of times, without glue. This will show you how much pressure is needed to push the tyre over and clear of the rim, so that the glue remains where it should be, rather than on the side walls of the tyres.

SPARES

I always carry an old, worn, spare that has some glue already on it. If you haven't got a used spare, spread some glue on a new tyre (and let it dry off completely) so that there is something to stick to, so you can get home in safety. Never ride on an unglued tyre, as this is very dangerous.

INSTALLATION

1 First of all, deflate the old tyre unless it's already punctured, and remove it by pushing it off and ripping it from the old glue. Cleaning the rim is essential – new aluminium rims can have oil and manufacturing cutting compounds still on the surface of the rim, and wheelbuilders will use oil on the spoke nipples. This oil will prevent the glue from sticking to the surface of the rim. Mountain bike disc-brake cleaner (Finish Line Speed Clean) is very good for this job, as it dries very quickly and there is no need to wash it off.

2 Used rims will have hard lumps of glue, and where these have collected there's a chance that they will prevent the tyre from rolling 'round'. The brake debris and road dirt can also prevent the tyre from sticking, so clean the whole wheel and allow time for it to dry off completely before you start to apply glue.

3 Use a wire brush on really stubborn old glue, and clean all the dust and debris away before you start to apply new glue. Be careful with carbon rims not to scratch the braking surface of the rim. Carbon rims need careful treatment, and be sure to check with the manufacturer as to their recommended choice of solvent and cleaning procedure.

4 Glue – most glues for tubulars are contact adhesives. This, somewhat obviously, means that they only work when two surfaces of pre-glued material are placed in contact with one another. Most of these glues work when they are dry or nearly dry (tacky) and once they have 'hardened' they are extremely resilient, especially to shearing forces, so they are perfect for keeping your tubs in place. My favourite glues are Continental, Vittoria and Tubasti – Continental is the most readily available and is very consistent and dries in next to no time.

5 Apply a layer of glue to the rim. There are a few ways to apply the glue to the rim – you can use your finger, but this is messy stuff, so I find the best way is with a 1/2in paintbrush (you can trim the bristles). Apply another coat of glue when the previous one has dried (no longer tacky).

Don't rush, but be careful to get the rim covered quickly. I find it's best to do this with the wheel in a wheel jig, so it is easy to rotate. If you don't have a jig, just upturn your bike and place the wheel in the forks or rear dropouts. Keep the glue well away from the spoke holes and try not to pool glue in places, as it drips easily.

6 Brush a coat of glue onto the underside of the tyre – the tub backing cloth covers the stitched part of the tyre and keeps it smooth for easy gluing to the rim. I usually do this with the tyre partially inflated and take care to spread the glue very evenly. On many tyres the first brush stroke will be absorbed into the cloth of the base tape, and some tyre tapes take more covering because of this, so most will need at least two coats of glue. Leave the tyre and rim for at least an hour to allow the glue to cure. I often leave the rim and tyre a little longer than an hour, as it's far easier to manipulate the longer you leave it.

7 Then apply a final coat of glue to the tyre only, not the rim. Then wait 10-20 minutes before starting to attach it. The glue should be almost dry again, but just a little tacky – make sure that there are no wet areas, especially on the tyre, as you are about to handle the glued part. Deflate the tyre once it's nearly dry and you're ready to install it.

8 With the wheel standing upright on a hard (non-carpeted!) floor, start by inserting the valve stem into the rim and seat the tyre on either side of the hole. Press firmly so that the tyre seats into the rim. Pull down with your hands to both sides, away from the stem, working around the rim, pressing and pushing very firmly, until reaching the bottom with only a short section of tyre not yet in place.

9 Lift the wheel and use your thumbs to push the remaining section onto the rim. To get the last section of tyre onto the rim without making a mess, grab the remaining four or five inches of tub and lift it away from, and over, the rim. If you struggle with this, flip the wheel over and hold the wheel at the valve hole onto the floor with your toes (take your shoes off for this!). You can then pull with your fingers rather than push with your thumbs.

10 Inflate the tyre enough for it to take some shape, and start to bed the tyre into the rim. Positioning the tyre can take a bit of patience, as there needs to be equal amounts of backing tape overlapping the edge of the rim. Flip the wheel several times to make sure that it is symmetrical.

11 The valve should be vertical in the rim hole and not angled, which makes it very hard to inflate and will also mean there is a high spot to the tyre where it is not seated correctly into the rim.

12 Spin the wheel to check for wobbles in the tyre tread and readjust until the tyre runs as true as possible before the glue starts to set.

13 Lastly, once you're happy that the glue is covered and the tyre is central to the rim, pump the tyres up to maximum pressure and leave for a minimum of 12 hours before you ride them.

TUBULAR TIPS

- Tubular tyres need to be pre-stretched before mounting. From new they should be stored unfolded and on a rim. Inflate them to around 80PSI and leave them in a wheel bag and out of direct sunlight. Leaving them inflated and on a rim will pre-stretch them enough to be glued onto the rim. Do not try to pull them into shape as this can break the stitching in the tubular carcass.

- Waterproofing can be applied to the sidewall of cotton tubulars. Aquaseal or a similar latex-based sealant can be used. This is especially popular with cyclo-cross tyres as the sidewall can be easily damaged and worn away. Treating it prevents water damage.

- Many race mechanics store tubular tyres for several seasons before they use them in competition, so that they 'mature' and the rubber will cure over time – meaning that they get tougher and less vulnerable to being penetrated by thorns and flints, yet will still retain their grip.

- Leaving any tyres in daylight is not a good idea, as the UV rays will damage the sidewall and lead to cracking. Keep spares in wheel bags and in a dry place. Once the tyre has started to crack or the tread is coming away from the carcass, the tyre is no longer much use.

- Old sprint rims are perfect for storing and pre-stretching tyres. It means that they are less likely to roll 'wonky' on the rim and they will require less pulling and forcing onto the rim when you come to glue them on.

- Most pro-track mechanics use a hard shellac-type glue and they need to be well installed to cope with the forces involved in cornering on a velodrome. I find Continental glue fine for track use, although I may add an extra coat of glue for peace of mind.

- Nail varnish remover (acetone) is very good for cleaning up, but be careful not to wipe it over the rim stickers, as it will remove them. Also check with the manufacturer (carbon rims especially) what solvents you can use.

- Keep (yourself) clean.

- During the process, clean off any glue from your hands with solvent as you go. Otherwise you will start to stick to the wheel and tyre too!

- I have used tub tape in emergencies, but it's not as good as glue. In fact most rolled tubs I have witnessed are because the rider has used tape and it has not adhered correctly to the tub or the rim. If you must use tub tape, make sure that the rim surface is completely degreased before you start.

- It is possible to repair a punctured tube, but this does involve a fair amount of skilled handiwork. Many lightweight tyres will be pretty useless for competition once they have been repaired too. Some companies will offer mail order repairs and they are worthwhile if the tyre is very new. Most tubulars only puncture when the casing is wearing through and/or the tyre is incorrectly inflated. So change tyres regularly and before the tread wears away – this will insure (as much as you can) against flats.

- To keep tubs in top condition it is best to deflate the tyre slightly after use, which prevents deformation of the tyre and prolongs tube life. The tubes are usually latex and will leak air over a short period of time. Like clincher tyres, they perform best when inflated to the correct pressure and allow some reduction in pressure for wet weather and rough road surfaces.

- Just like clinchers, tubs need to have regular tread inspections for flints and shards of glass that may work their way into the carcass and put an end to your day's riding. Deflate the tyre and flick out any debris with a sharp awl, and always replace the tub if the cuts mean the tube is exposed.

05

FRAME

Building a bike from scratch is a hugely rewarding process. However, you'll only be able to do it properly – and it'll only save you money – if you have the right tools. Much of the following chapter relies on specialist tools that only a bike shop will have access to. However, if you are buying a new frame to build up yourself, consider these steps before you part with any money. A good shop will fit bottom brackets, forks and Aheadsets for you, especially if you buy them from the same place, so it's always worth asking. Remember that a well-prepared frame is a solid foundation for both the components and the rider.

FRAME ALIGNMENT

Frame alignment is the first step to building your perfect bike. The head tube and seat tube have to be in line in order for the bike to handle properly, and the rear dropouts have to be positioned so that they hold the rear wheel directly behind the front wheel. This is called frame track. Crashing can cause invisible damage to bikes, so track should be regularly checked out. Use some of the following steps, as they'll help you identify problems and damage. This assessment is essential if you want to keep safe and prevent further accidents, should components or frames fail.

1 The Park frame alignment tool used here makes alignment assessment easier. The tool rests on the head tube and seat tube, and the pointer gauge is adjusted to sit on the outside of the dropout. The gauge is then set and flipped over to the other side. If the bike is symmetrical, the gauge won't have to be re-adjusted.

TOOLS REQUIRED

- **M5 taps and tapping wrench**
- **Cutting paste**
- **Cleaning kit, including rags and degreaser/spray lube**
- **Frame alignment tool**
- **Rear dropout alignment tool**
- **Rear mech alignment tool**
- **String**
- **Ruler**
- **Vernier callipers**

2 For a far safer quick check, you just need a long piece of string. Wrap it around the head tube and trap either end under the QR skewer, or get someone to hold it, while you measure the string. The string needs to be very taut and the wheel should be in place for an accurate reading.

3 The critical measurement will be between the seat tube and either side of the length of string.

A difference of 1–2mm is acceptable and won't affect the bike's handling. However, if you've crashed and the measurement is more than 4–5mm, the frame may require attention from either a qualified framebuilder or the manufacturer.

4 The dropout alignment tools shown here are used to check that the rear end is correctly spaced and aligned for the rear wheel. With the dropout tools fully inserted in the drop out, the central sections can be adjusted to meet in the middle. If they don't meet up, the dropouts have been twisted. These tools are long so that the mechanic can 'cold set' (bend) them slightly to meet perfectly.

5 Measure across the dropouts between the inner faces. Road bikes are 130mm. Mountain bike hubs are 135mm, while single-speed hubs and BMX hubs can be 110mm, 115mm or 120mm. A narrower gap will make removing the wheels a little trickier, and over-wide dropouts can distort the rear end when you clamp up the QR lever.

6 It's essential to face the bottom bracket shell and the head tube. This is explained in the Aheadsets and bottom bracket sections (see pages 96-100), but it's important to remember that if you don't have these tools, the bike shop should prepare the frame for you.

7 Getting the right bottom bracket is essential too. Measure across the bottom bracket faces and butt the appropriate unit, which should be 68mm. Some mountain bike and touring frames are 73mm. Fitting the wrong size will alter the chainline and mess up your shifting. See pages 94-95 for more on bottom brackets and page 188-189 for more on chainlines.

8 Bottle-bolt bosses get bunged up with paint and, on steel frames, can rust up. Aluminium frames have riveted bottle bosses, which can be replaced with a specialist tool. Tap out

the threads before you attach a bottle cage with an M5 tap. Be careful not to go too far. You'll need the same-size tool for rack fittings and cable guides as well, so it's worth buying one.

9 The rear mech hanger is possibly the most vulnerable part of the road bike frame. Many frames have replaceable hangers, which may require replacing after a serious crash. Simply unbolt the replaceable part and order a new one from your dealer. However, if you've dropped your bike, there may be a slight bend in the hangers. This can play merry hell with your gearshift. The rear mech alignment tool used here allows you to check and cold set the gear hanger.

10 Once you've screwed the tool into the dropout, you can position it at several points around the wheel. The gauges on the tool allow you to lock it off using the wheel rim as a reference. If the gap between the gauges varies, you'll have to adjust the dropout until there's a uniform gap all around. Perfect shifting can only be achieved with a straight mech, so check this after every stack. If you've bent an aluminium dropout several times, you'll need to replace it as it may snap. Once you've 'set' the hanger you can replace the rear mech.

11 Finally, remember to cover the frame at the points that rub on the cables and place a chainstay protector under the chain. These vulnerable positions will wear through the paint in no time, usually on the first ride. Neoprene protectors are a good idea, as the chain literally bounces off them.

FRAME PREPARATION

BOTTOM BRACKETS (BBS)

This process cleans out any paint, rust and material from the threads in the shell and ensures that the threads are running parallel. The facing element means that the unit will tighten up square.

A square edge to the BB shell is very important, as the life of the bottom bracket bearings will be greatly improved if they sit square to the frame and to the cranks – they'll also be noise-free and the BB unit will be easier to remove.

Clean out the frame's bottom bracket shell thoroughly with a degreaser and dry it off. Then dress all the threads with plenty of anti-seize or quality synthetic grease. The bottom bracket is often neglected for many months, so how easy it is to remove depends on how well it was prepared before it was put in.

TOOLS REQUIRED

- **Bottom bracket tool**
- **Torque wrench**
- **Quality thread cutters**
- **Facing tool**
- **Cutting paste**
- **Cleaning fluid (or degreaser)**
- **Callipers or ruler (for measuring bottom bracket and shell)**
- **8mm crank Allen key**
- **Anti-seize compound or synthetic grease**

1 Before you start, you may have to remove the plastic cable guide bolt from under the bottom bracket shell, as it'll snag on the cutters when they run through the threads. The tool will have the thread type stamped onto the cutters for identification, but double-check that you have the right cutters before you use them.

2 Tap the threads using a quality in-line tap set. Remember that the drive-side or right crank is a left-hand thread (tightens anti-clockwise) and the non-drive-side or left crank is a right-hand thread (tightens clockwise). Push the two sides of the cutting tool towards the edges of the BB shell and keep them straight.

3 Standing behind the bike you can rotate the cutters correctly by pushing down with both hands. (If you have Italian threads, do not do this, as they're both right-hand threads!) Turn the cutters gradually and evenly – don't force them in, as they should cut into the threads easily. If they start to seize up, there may be an obstruction in the shell. Use plenty of cutting paste and keep turning until the cutters sit flush into the frame.

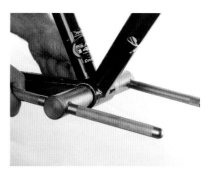

4 Once you've tapped the threads, you can face the right-hand edge of the bottom bracket. These Park tools have a central spigot so you can use it as a thread cutter and a facing tool, so leave the thread cutter in on the opposite side, as it maintains the accurate alignment of the facing tool.

5 When you're using the facing tool, you'll need plenty of cutting paste. The cutters need consistent pressure to prevent them from 'chattering' and damaging the edge. Remember not to run the tool backwards as this can damage the cutter.

6 Keep a close eye on the bracket face and check that it's clear of paint and completely square (when properly faced it should look smooth and shiny all over).

7 Regularly strip and redress the BB threads. Black aluminium oxides can build up and create problems. The best way to remove these is with a brass brush and a little de-greaser.

8 The left-hand side of the BB may be left unfaced if you're using a standard BB that has a non-flanged BB cup on the non-drive side. Through-axle-style BBs (Campagnolo Ultra Torque and Shimano Hollowtech II) will need both faces of the BB shell cutting and faced flush, as they have external bearing cups that both need to thread in parallel and square.

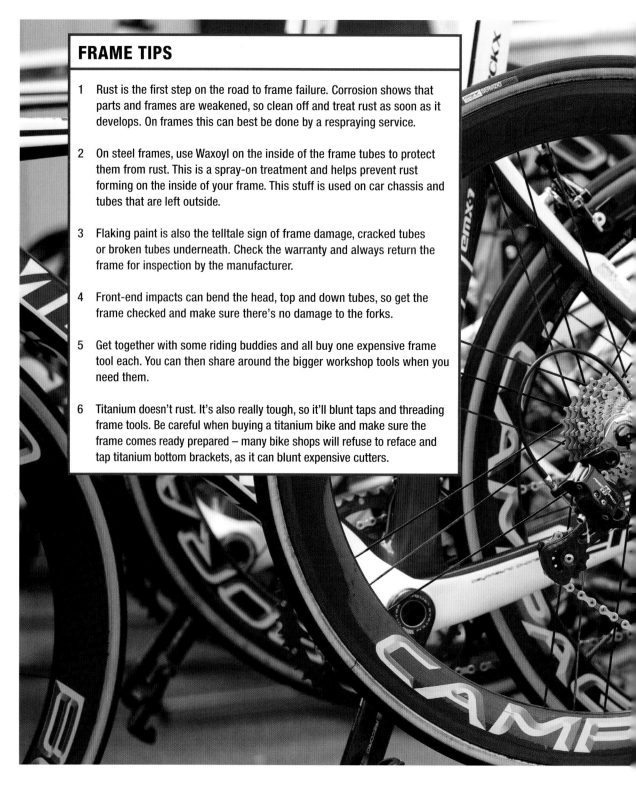

FRAME TIPS

1   Rust is the first step on the road to frame failure. Corrosion shows that parts and frames are weakened, so clean off and treat rust as soon as it develops. On frames this can best be done by a respraying service.

2   On steel frames, use Waxoyl on the inside of the frame tubes to protect them from rust. This is a spray-on treatment and helps prevent rust forming on the inside of your frame. This stuff is used on car chassis and tubes that are left outside.

3   Flaking paint is also the telltale sign of frame damage, cracked tubes or broken tubes underneath. Check the warranty and always return the frame for inspection by the manufacturer.

4   Front-end impacts can bend the head, top and down tubes, so get the frame checked and make sure there's no damage to the forks.

5   Get together with some riding buddies and all buy one expensive frame tool each. You can then share around the bigger workshop tools when you need them.

6   Titanium doesn't rust. It's also really tough, so it'll blunt taps and threading frame tools. Be careful when buying a titanium bike and make sure the frame comes ready prepared – many bike shops will refuse to reface and tap titanium bottom brackets, as it can blunt expensive cutters.

PRO TIPS

1   Titanium frames will (well, should) have been properly prepared at the factory. Few cutters are capable of cutting titanium easily and you'll blunt a steel cutter very quickly if you try – it's very tough stuff. Also, when assembling any threaded titanium components, remember to use copper slip (Ti-Prep) as it'll prevent materials from seizing completely. If a titanium frame needs facing, take it to a specialist framebuilder who'll have the right tools.

2   Be careful with carbon, as facing the BB shell may mean cutting into glue and fibres around the BB shell – this can jeopardise the frame's strength, and it's certainly worth getting a pro shop mechanic to assess your frame before trying to face carbon shells. Most carbon frames have aluminium inserts that can be faced, but do take care when cutting carbon.

HEADSETS AND AHEADSETS

The Aheadset is a very simple component and the unit is therefore relatively easy to maintain and service. The system consists of two bearing races positioned at either end of the head tube. The races run in these bearings and are trapped by the fork at one end and the stem at the other. The stem clamps the system together and prevents it from coming loose. A well-prepared head tube and a properly fitted Aheadset will help the unit last longer. Even the cheaper Aheadsets on the market can last a long time if your bike is properly prepared and the unit is serviced regularly.

TYPES OF AHEADSET
1IN OR 11/8IN

Bicycle fork steerers were 1in in diameter for many years. Before Aheadset forks, steerers were threaded into the headset, but the threaded type is now rare (see page 102 for more). Most road bikes now have a 11/8in Aheadset, which is becoming the industry standard.

AHEADSET CUPS

Aheadset cups can be made from steel, aluminium or titanium. Aluminium cups are still the most popular and titanium cups are lightweight but quite pricey. There's one brand that stands apart from the rest – Chris King. I've had King Aheadsets that have lasted longer than the frames they were fitted into – they're superb.

INTEGRATED OR HIDDEN AHEADSETS

Integrated Aheadsets have the bearings pressed directly into the frame. The factory will have fitted these, and the quality of the framebuilding is always going to dictate how good this will be. There's usually a flare at the top and bottom of the head tube to accept the bearing parts. In my experience, standard head tubes are better because they allow easier servicing and can be easier to find replacements for.

STIFFER FRONT END?

Generally speaking, shorter, slimmer head tubes do put more strain on the bearings than long ones. However, the latest design of 'integrated' head tubes can be made bigger, and therefore (generally speaking) make for a stiffer front end.

CARBON STEERERS AND FORKS

Take care with carbon components. Forks need careful checking after a crash.

BASIC AHEADSET ADJUSTMENT

1 To check the Aheadset, apply the front brake, and rock the bike backwards and forwards. You'll feel

or hear a slight knocking if the unit is loose. If you've been running the unit loose for a while, the chances are that the bearings will need replacing – riding with a loose Aheadset will batter the bearings and ruin the surfaces in the unit.

2 It's also possible that the system is too tight or notchy. To check this, pick up the front of the bike and let the bars hang under their own weight. Stiff head parts won't budge. If the Aheadset is too tight it's unlikely that it'll flop to one side, as shown here. A properly adjusted Aheadset with smooth bearings should have no play and be able to move easily, as shown.

3 Loosen the two bolts on the side of the stem. These bolts clamp the stem to the top of the steerer and also keep the Aheadset unit complete.

4 Once you've loosened the bolts, tighten the top cap slightly (this preloads it) to take up any play in the system. You'll only need a small nip to tighten the unit (around 3Nm). If you're removing the top cap and fork as well as the Aheadset, be aware that the fork will be free to fall out once the clamp is undone and the top cap removed.

5 Retighten the stem-clamp bolts to the recommended torque setting. Always use a torque wrench to check the final time, especially if you're using a carbon steerer and/or stem.

SERVICING

If you're servicing the Aheadset bearings, remove the bars and disconnect the front brake so that the forks can be removed and set aside (if you're fitting forks and a new Aheadset, see page 104).

1 The bearings will either be a sealed cartridge or ball bearings, as shown here. Both systems are good, but the advantage with loose bearings is that they can be stripped out and re-greased. The advantage with cartridge-type bearings is that they can be completely replaced. If the bearings are wearing out regularly, the cups could be out of line in the frame and they'll therefore need to be refitted. See page 104 for how to prepare a head tube.

2 Once you've serviced the bearings, the forks can be re-installed. Make sure that you return all the seals the right way up, and that

you grease the bearings and insert them into the cups the right way around. Don't leave the forks in the bike without returning the stem, even if the friction in the seals appears to be enough to hold them in place.

3 There should be a gap between the top of the steerer and the inside top of the Aheadstem of approximately 2–3mm. The gap shouldn't be any bigger than this, as the Aheadstem bolts must be able to tighten over the steerer. If the bolts are above the height of the steerer, the stem will be distorted and won't be tightened to the correct torque figure. The problem isn't just that you might pull the bars off, but the stem will also loosen over time and damage the bearings. See page 104 for more on installing the Aheadset properly.

4 When you replace the top cap, check that the bottom of the top cap doesn't snag on the top of the steerer. If it does, you may have to place an extra spacer on top of the stem to give a little more space.

5 Most stems have two clamp bolts, one on either side, so that the stem won't be pulled over to one side as you tighten the bolts. It's critical that you don't over- or under-tighten these bolts. Retighten the stem clamp bolts to the manufacturer's recommended torque settings – which will be adequate and will mean that the bars will still twist in the event of a crash.

6 Before refitting the handlebars, check that there are no sharp edges around the stem clamp. Also check that you have the right diameter bars and stem. Standard road stems are 26.0mm, but the latest size ('oversize') is 31.8mm. Most decent handlebar stems, such as the one pictured here, have slightly chamfered edges. Put a dab of copper slip on the stem bolts before replacing them, to prevent them from seizing.

7 Replace the front section of the bar clamp. Number the bolts 1–4 clockwise, then tighten them alternately (e.g. 1–3– 2–4) and to 6–7 Nm. Don't over-tighten the bolts or tighten them too quickly – make sure you reach the desired torque setting gradually. Line the handlebars up and make sure that you've positioned them centrally. See pages 152-5 for more on handlebar set-up.

8 Once you've tightened the stem, check that there's an equal gap at the top and bottom between the clamping sections. If there's a difference, tighten or loosen the stem bolts until they match. This is critical, as it'll ensure that there's an equal force on each bolt and that the bar is properly clamped. This is especially important with carbon bars and light-weight aluminium ones.

9 Check that the bars are straight and that the stem is tight. Line the bars up with the front hub. You can hold the wheel between your legs and line the bars up by twisting them. You may need to loosen the stem bolts slightly to make this possible. Recheck the play – if the Aheadset remains tight and you've tried resetting the stem bolts, it's likely that one of the bearings or weather seals has been inserted the wrong way, so check this and re-tighten using a Torque wrench and the manufacturer's recommended torque settings.

STANDARD HEADSETS AND STEMS

Standard headsets share similar parts to Aheadsets, especially the frame cups. Installation of the basic frame parts is the same. The main difference is the fitting to the forks and how the stem attaches to the fork.

Headset types for road bikes are fewer than for mountain bikes. Road bikes never had 1 1/8in standard-sized headsets with quill stems – they changed straight over to 1in and 1 1/8in-sized Aheadsets, with 1 1/8in taking over as the 'industry standard' soon after. A few manufacturers have stuck with the standard non-integrated-headset look (Seven, Serotta and Colnago) and there's a lot to be said for the standard system (easier to replace and more reliable), although the current trend for smooth integrated head tubes and forks appears to be taking over. Standard quill stems and headsets are now rare, and while there's nothing wrong with them and they work just as well, they require some specialist headset spanners to adjust. The quill stem is less serviceable than an Aheadset, as it's harder to remove the bars without removing the tape and the brake levers. However, the best thing about quill stems is that they offer larger ranges of adjustment than the Aheadset system.

1 The quill stem is held in place with a wedge system that traps the shaft of the stem inside the fork steerer. A 6mm Allen key holds the wedge tight in the end of the stem.

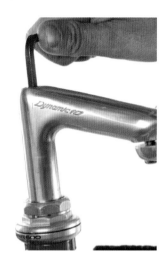

2 Even after the bolt is undone, the stem stays wedged in place – don't undo the bolt completely, but just enough so that the head of the bolt protrudes from the stem.

3 Tap the top of the bolt gently with a plastic mallet, or use a piece of wood to protect the head of the bolt and use a standard hammer.

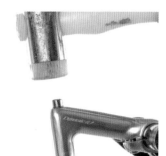

4 The quill stem system has plenty of adjustment for height, but there's a minimum-insert limit line marked and you mustn't go beyond this. It's worth noting that the height range available with a quill stem is far greater than an Aheadset system.

5 The bolt travels the length of the stem and the wedge is attached to the bottom. It's important not to undo the bolt too far, as the wedge can fall into the stem.

6 The standard 1in headset requires two 32mm headset spanners to undo the locknut. The bottom one traps the forks and prevents them from spinning, then the locknut can be removed.

7 The locknut threads onto the fork steerer, and there's a washer underneath, between the steerer and the top locking nut.

8 The top race sits directly on top of the bearings, which in turn sit inside the top cup. To service the system properly, you'll need to remove the forks and access the bearings at both ends of the headset.

9 The threaded part of steerer has to be cut precisely (as with Aheadsets on page 104). This Shimano headset has a sealed bearing unit that can be replaced. Campagnolo headsets (and Aheadsets) still use ball bearings held in cages, which can be cleaned, re-greased and replaced.

10 Adjustment is simple but requires the right tools. Once the top race has been threaded onto the forks and nipped up, the locking top nut and washer can be screwed on and into place. Balancing the play and free-running bearing is a question of tightening the race and backing it off against the locking nut.

11 Once you've finished servicing the headset, make sure that you clean and grease the inside of the fork steerer and the wedge-and-quill arrangement before you re-install the stem.

FORK INSTALLATION

To install Aheadsets correctly, you need to prepare your frame carefully and to have some specialist tools. Often, the bike shop will fit the forks and therefore do this preparation work for you, but if you need to do it yourself, it's important to follow the steps below – your bike will ride better and last longer if you do.

Titanium frames won't usually require the facing and cleaning-out process, as this should've been done in the factory when the frame was made. Carbon frames should also have been faced properly. As always, consult the manufacturer's instructions or ask your local dealer if you are unsure.

FORK RAKE

Road bikes are designed to be used with a specific fork. Fitting the wrong fork can change the steering characteristics quite drastically. Most forks will have their rake marked on them somewhere – it's the measurement from the centre line of the head tube to the centre of the fork's dropout, which is pretty tricky to measure with a ruler, but:

- 40mm is intended for track use and some TT bikes
- 43mm or 45mm are the standard road bike rakes – which one is used will vary according to frame-size/design
- 55mm may be used on some cyclo-cross bikes and touring bikes, for comfort and slower steering characteristics.

1 Old headset cups can be removed with a cup-removing tool like this one, which splays out inside the head tube and ensures a snug fit on the inside of the cups. It rests on top of the cups and allows you to tap it out with equal force. Using a long screwdriver is not an option, as it can damage the inside of the frame and ruin the cups.

2 Tap the cup-removing tool with a mallet to remove the cups. With some smaller head tubes it can be tricky to get the tool to fit properly, as the jaws can be restricted by the other race. So, be careful and make sure you wrap a cloth around the cup to prevent it pinging off around the workshop.

STACK HEIGHT

I've already mentioned that Aheadsets come in a variety of different sizes (1in, 1 1/8in and 1 1/2in), but each manufacturer makes them with a different stack height too. Stack height is the amount of space that the cups take up on the steerer. If you are fitting a new Aheadset, make sure that you buy a similar make or one with the same stack height. If the stack is too high, the stem won't have enough steerer to hold on to. Remember that most forks will be ruined if you cut the steerer too short, as they can't be replaced – so always double-check your measurements before you cut.

3 The crown race is a very delicate component and can also be slightly smaller than the crown of most forks, which can make it difficult to remove. You can remove some crown races by tapping them with a plastic mallet and a suitably soft drift, but it's far better to use a crown race-removing tool, as it won't scratch the forks and damage the crown.

5 When you've faced the tube, it'll look perfectly flat and shiny like this one, and the Aheadset cups will fit squarely into the tube. Clean out all the swarf from the inside and grease the top and bottom faces with some anti-seize grease. Grease the inner parts of the cups too, and check they're the right way up (the logos are usually a dead giveaway).

7 It's best to do one cup at a time to avoid damage and so you can line up the logos. Some cups have grease-guard ports, which should face to the side so you can get to them easily. The tool simply (and quickly) forces the cups into the head tube – don't try to install a headset with a hammer, as this won't work.

4 The tool pictured here is a dual-purpose cutter. It faces the head tube and also cuts the inside of the tube at the same time, making sure that the Aheadset cups are inserted squarely into the tube. The top and the bottom of the tube are faced – this is to ensure that the cups are parallel so they don't work against each other and wear out quickly. It'll remove any rust or paint on the tube and also make sure the cups are a perfect fit.

6 Remove any seals from the cups, as they may get damaged as the cup is pressed in. Insert the cup so that it's straight and can't distort as you push it in with the headset press tool – the cups usually have a shamfered edge to guide them into the tube.

8 Now the top cup can go in. The tool has a variety of dies that fit different sized cups. Make sure that you use one that fits well but not too snugly, as the force on the tool can make it seize onto the aluminium cup and ruin it. You'll find that the cups will be easier to install if the head tube has been cut and faced. Finally, inspect the cups closely to check that they're flush with the tube (hold the bike up to the light and see if there are any gaps).

CUTTING FORKS

1 It's best to measure the old fork steerer with a ruler first and then compare it with the old forks once you've marked them, otherwise you'll have to assemble the whole system before cutting the new fork. This is essential if you are changing position or fitting a different type of Aheadset or stem.

2 Mark the steerer with a permanent marker pen, as you'll have to insert the forks into the head tube before it's cut. Alternatively, use a vernier calliper and measure the amount you need to remove, then add 2mm to account for the recess required to fit the top cap.

3 Next, fit the fork crown race. Most forks will have factory-cut crowns, but some need facing for a perfect fit – there's a workshop tool to do this job if necessary, which knocks the crown race onto the crown – make sure that the adaptor is a good fit to the race and remove any rubber or plastic seals before you do this, as they can be damaged.

4 At this point, assemble the complete system, including bearings, to check you have the steerer at the right length. Although you may not want to cut the steerer twice, it may be better If you're not sure how high you want the bars.

5 It's better to allow for more spacers if you are unsure how high you want your bars. If I'm assembling a bike for someone else, I always leave 30mm of spacers under the stem so that the rider can decide. The steerer can always be cut again after a test ride.

6 Cut the steerer to length using a sharp new hacksaw blade, holding the steerer in a cutting guide to stop the blade wandering as you cut. It's essential that the cut is square to ensure that the stem fits properly and the 'star nut' (see step 8) can be installed easily. If you are cutting a carbon-fibre steerer, wear a face mask.

7 File off any burrs on the outside and inside of the steerer tube with a half-round file. Take care not to scratch the steerer and make sure that the edges of the tube won't scratch the inside of the stem when you replace it. The inside has to be clear so that the top cap nut can be easily inserted inside the tube.

8 On steel and aluminium steerers, the star nut is the fixed part of the system and allows the stem top cap to fasten down on the headset stack, and allows you to adjust out any play in the system. They're not recommended for carbon-fibre steerers and may be difficult to fit to some aluminium steerers with thicker tube walls.

10 Once inserted, star nuts are very hard to remove, as they fit by wedging themselves into the inside of the tube. This scratches the tube, so removing the nut can make a big mess of both the nut and the steerer. If the star-fangled nut is damaged or seized, simply knock it further down the steerer and fit a replaceable wedge.

12 Once tightened into the steerer, these units are safer and can be refitted, which is really important if you don't have a star nut setting tool. They also can't damage the inside of the steerer tube, so can be used on carbon steerers. But, best of all, they're also less likely to rust and seize, as you can remove them and clean them up.

9 Use a star nut setting tool, as pictured here, and you can't fail to get it set straight in the steerer.

11 Alternatively (and more favourably), you can use a replaceable top cap and wedge. I prefer to use one of these removable top-cap wedges – these units are inserted and tightened into the steerer with an Allen key.

13 Expandable wedges like this are essential in carbon steerers as star nuts can damage carbon steerers irreparably.

14 The stem must fit with a recess of 2–3mm of steerer – this allows for adjustment and for the top cap to fit. Then adjust the stem and tighten all the bolts to the recommended torque settings.

FITTING MUDGUARDS

Whatever kind of bike you choose to ride in the winter, mudguards (fenders in the USA) are a great idea when you don't need to be too concerned about weight. Wet winter-weather riding with mudguards means that your backside and feet will remain dry and you can ride in comfort. Fitting them can be a bit of a fiddle, especially if the bike has tight clearances at the rear wheel.

Shorter mudguards are now available for racing frames and these will offer a level of rain protection, but nothing beats full mudguard cover, so if you have to commute in all weathers and/or train in Northern Europe – get some mudguards!

Also be aware that shallow-rake racing forks may not be suitable for mudguards and a safe toe-overlap to the front wheel. Always check that you can turn the handlebars and pedal without causing pedal-overlap problems.

1 Frames designed to accommodate mudguards (or a rack) will usually be supplied with eyelets for 5mm threaded bolts – this is the best way to secure the 'guards safely and securely.

2 Fit the stays to the threaded eyelet on the dropout. Use a stainless steel bolt and washer to prevent the bolt rattling free, and so as not to spread the stays as you tighten it up.

3 Front-wheel mudguards come with these clips attached to the end that will break away in an emergency, preventing the guards from catching in the front wheel.

4 If you're fitting 'guards to a fork without threaded bosses, these plastic-coated brackets or P-clips allow you to fit mudguards to bikes without brazed-on fittings at the dropouts. They can also be used to attach four-point fixing racks to the back of the bike.

5 The front 'guard has a brake-bracket tab ready fitted to it. This is slotted over the brake bolt and can be adjusted for height away from the tyre.

6 If the frame has no threaded hole under the brake bridge, use this metal clip to secure the rear 'guard under the rear brake (these are usually supplied with the 'guards).

7 Once the rear 'guard has been slotted through this clip and secured at the chainstay bridge, you can crimp the metal clip into place with some needle-nose pliers.

8 However, securing the rear mudguard to the brake bridge is best done with a bolt threaded into the bridge itself, and many frames have a hole here ready drilled and tapped.

9 This is an Allen-key bolt holding the 'guard in place. It's the best way to secure the 'guards firmly, and prevent them rubbing on the tyres and rattling as you ride.

10 Some frames can have mudguard attachments built into the seat tube – these are a good idea on tighter clearance frames and carbon frames, like this one, that don't have a bridge behind the bottom bracket between the chainstays.

11 Most frame-fitting mudguards clip on to the bridge behind the bottom bracket – as with the brake-bridge fitting, this can have a threaded hole in it.

12 The stays are attached to the mudguard with a bolt that has a hole through it. The stay has to pass through this in order to secure the 'guard with an 8mm spanner.

13 Firstly, just tighten the bolts slightly. Nip them up so that they can still be moved by hand to position them over the wheel. Do not bend the stays to get them centred – adjusting the 'guards by loosening the stay bolts is far easier.

14 Finish off the cut end of the stay with a plastic cover – this prevents the sharp end catching on clothing.

FULL MUDGUARDS FIT BEST TO BIKES WITH
ADEQUATE CLEARANCE IN THE FRAME –
LIKE THIS CONDOR WINTER TRAINING BIKE

06

GEARS

A 10-speed racer was once the pinnacle of bicycle technology. Index systems and the improvements made to hubs and mechs (derailleurs) has meant that larger gear ratios and wider spreads of gears are easily available. Nowadays, most new bikes come with nine- or 10-speed cassettes and two or three chainwheels to provide anything from 18 to 30 gear ratios. Cassettes and chains are designed to work smoothly and shift crisply, which means that they're complicated and finely engineered, and therefore susceptible to wear and tear. Changing cassettes is necessary for changes in terrain and types of riding (racing, training, touring) and although a cassette will last for a season or so (if you keep replacing the chain), it will wear out in the end.

CASSETTES AND GEAR RATIOS

STANDARD CASSETTE RATIOS

11–21

A racing ratio for mainly flat courses, time trials and for sprinter-roadmen, this is not a cassette ratio for hilly rides or long training weekends in the Alps. Usually used by specialists with standard 53/39 chainsets for racing only.

11–23 OR 12–23

A good all-round racing ratio, suitable for quick, slightly hilly circuits. This is the standard road riding/racing ratio and can be used with either standard or Compact chainsets.

12–25

Better suited to hillier circuits. This is the ratio that most professional riders use in the Alps and Pyrenees during the Tour de France (though usually with a 39-tooth inner chainring!). For we lesser mortals with less painful ambitions, this also combines very well with Compact ratios.

13–29

The choice ratio for riding in the high mountains (for those in the know). It's also the main choice for Challenge rides, gran fondos, 'centuries' and the Etape du Tour. Works best with Compact (I like the 50/36 crank here) and it gives almost as many options as a triple chainset. If you decide to use 13–29, it's likely you'll need a mid- or long-cage mech, depending on your set-up. (Please see rear mech section beginning on page 120 for details on this.)

MAVIC

Mavic's own system is slightly different again – their M10 cassette can be used in a variety of combinations, as each cog is individually mounted. I like this system, as it's totally customised and supplied with nine- and 10-speed spacer kits for use with either Campagnolo gear system. (An eight-speed Campagnolo spacer kit is available as an option.)

It's also possible to buy a Shimano-compatible nine-speed spacer kit for Mavic wheels. There are other aftermarket cassettes that allow you to use Campagnolo gears with Shimano hubs and vice versa – Marchisio make such a system and Royce make spacers to help customisation from nine-speed back to eight-speed – so almost anything is possible.

FREEHUB BODY

All cassette configurations fit a freehub body that is attached to the rear hub. These have a set of shaped keyways and slots that allow the cassette sprockets to engage and stay in contact with the hub. This also orientates the sprockets as the teeth have one way to face and a sequence of ramps and cutaways to ensure smooth shifting.

STANDARD CHAINSET (CRANK) CONFIGURATIONS

Type	Number of teeth Big/small rings
Compact	48/36, 50/36 or 50/34
Triple	30/42/52
Standard double	52/42 or 53/39

Read the sections on cranks and Compact drive in chapter 9 to find out more about cranks and chainrings.

CASSETTE RATIOS AVAILABLE (SHIMANO AND CAMPAGNOLO)

- Campagnolo 10-speed cassettes usually come in the following ratios: 11–21; 11–23; 11–25; 12–23; 12–25; 13–26; 13–29.

- Campagnolo nine-speed cassettes are now less common, but usually come in: 12–23; 13–23; 13–26.

- Shimano nine- and 10-speed cassettes are usually available in: 11–21; 11–23; 12–21; 12–23; 12–25; 12–27.

This is a guide only, as many other custom ratios are possible – some people do use mountain bike cassettes with road groups, which can make up to 32 teeth possible, and may be useful for touring bikes.

CASSETTE SERVICE AND REPLACEMENT

REMOVING CASSETTES (SHIMANO AND CAMPAGNOLO)

1 Cassette servicing is best done with the wheel intact and the tyres still attached to the rim (in case you have to rest the wheel on the floor or lean on it for extra purchase).

2 The cassette lock-ring tool fits into the serrated inside of the lock-ring. Shimano and Campagnolo use the same principle, but not the same tool!

TOOLS REQUIRED

- **Chain whip**
- **Cassette lock-ring tool and spanner/wrench**
- **Torque wrench**

3 The standard socket-type tool can be held in place with the QR skewer to prevent it from rounding off the cassette lock-ring or slipping and causing injury or damage.

4 This double-sided tool also features a central locating pin (it's a personal favourite of mine!). It means you can use it with either system, and the pin helps hold the tool in place and allows for a firmer grip.

5 Remove the cassette using a chain whip and cassette lock-ring removal tool. The chain whip prevents the cassette from turning (freewheeling), and should be positioned so that the chain on the tool can wrap around the sprocket enough to prevent it from spinning when you push on the wrench.

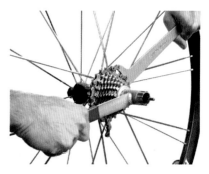

6 Campagnolo 10-speed requires a chain whip with a 10-speed chain end to prevent damage to the sprockets and slipping as you apply pressure.

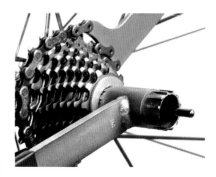

7 Shimano systems can use a standard chain whip. Stand over the wheel with the cassette facing away from you. Hold the chain whip in your left hand and the lock-ring tool in your right. Set the whip over the second-biggest gear and position the tools as shown. Pushing down with both hands will undo the lock-ring.

8 The first two or three cassette sprockets will be loose, so be careful not to drop them. Lay the wheel flat on the workbench and take the sprockets off one by one, placing them down in the order in which they came off the wheel.

SHIMANO NINE-SPEED AND 10-SPEED SET-UPS

1 Apply a thin layer of grease or anti-seize to the cassette body before you slide the cassette back into place. This will prevent the cassette body from rusting. If there's any corrosion on the body, use a brass suede-shoe brush to clean it off.

2 The lock-ring threads into the cassette body and secures the sprockets. Because the cassette is integral to the drive, this needs to be tight.

3 Spacers may be required on some wheelsets, especially when they're not Shimano. Bear this in mind if you're setting up the gears too, as it can change the spacing and therefore the indexing for the rear mech.

4 Better-quality Shimano cassettes have the first few large cassette sprockets attached to a 'spider' or aluminium carrier to save some weight without losing rigidity.

5 The remaining cassette sprockets are loose and have a spacer (marked nine- or 10-speed) to ensure the correct spacing and alignment of the sprockets.

6 The serrated teeth pressed into the last sprocket and the underside of the lock-ring prevent it from vibrating loose.

SPROCKETS: CAMPAGNOLO 10-SPEED HUBS

1 Like Shimano, Campagnolo has a special cassette body that orientates the cassette sprockets. They also come in a variety of materials and qualities.

2 Between the first and second cluster of sprockets, Campagnolo use a wider spacer that also has a larger outside diameter.

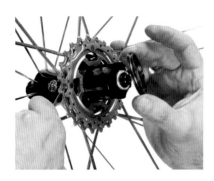

3 The second pair of sprockets are also held on a carrier – in Record, these first two clusters are made from titanium.

4 When the first four gears are in place, there's another special wider-diameter spacer to put in place before the smaller single loose sprockets can be added.

5 Like Shimano, the smaller set of sprockets will have single spacers between each one.

6 The final two sprockets may not require the spacers, as they're ready machined with the spacer attached, and the last sprocket will have serrations on the outside to keep it tight up against the lock-ring.

SPROCKETS: CAMPAGNOLO NINE-SPEED HUBS

The better-quality nine-speed units are the same as 10-speed to install, although the cheaper-quality cassettes can have simple plastic spacers and are less complicated to install. However, they both fit the same Campagnolo nine-/10-speed pattern hubs.

ALL SYSTEMS

Once the cassette system is in place, tighten the lock-ring to 35–50Nm. You'll be surprised how tight this is, but the cassette bears a considerable load and needs to be checked for tightness regularly.

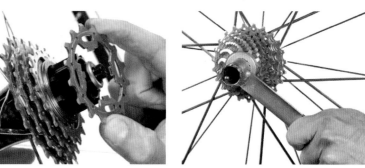

CASSETTE TOP TIPS

1   A new cassette means you'll need a new chain – chains wear out and will slip on brand new sprockets.

2   Keep expensive titanium and aluminium cassettes for race days and mountain climbing only – they last better and will perform for many years if only given the odd outing.

3   Train on steel sprockets and replace them regularly.

4   Clean the sprockets with a good degreaser each time you swap them over and brush between the tight spaces that you can't reach when the cassette is assembled.

5   Although SRAM cassette sprockets do work with Shimano hubs (and vice versa), they won't fit on new Dura Ace cassette bodies and will only fit older Shimano hubs.

6   Cassette carriers come with SRAM, Miche and Campagnolo cassettes – these are plastic clips that line up with the cassette body's grooves.

7   These will allow you to simply slide the sprockets into place without having to replace each one individually, which will prevent you from missing out spacers or dropping them all on the floor.

REAR MECHS (DERAILLEURS) AND INDEX SYSTEMS

Derailleur is the official name for these components, but most people call them mechs – so that's the term that I've used in this book. Mechs are essentially guide plates for the chain that allow it to be moved onto the next chainwheel. Most fit to the seat tube with a clamp.

The modern rear mech gear has an index system. Shimano were the first company to successfully market one, the SIS (Shimano Index System). Usually, this is a seven-, eight-, nine- or 10-speed set-up. A ratchet in the gear lever allows one gear or multiple gears to be shifted with very little effort. One click of the gear lever pulls the cables a preset amount, relative to the distance the mech has to move to hop the chain one sprocket on. This is very efficient, but relies on the cables staying put. In time, the cable will stretch and this slight movement throws the whole system out of whack.

SHIMANO STI (SHIMANO TOTAL INTEGRATION) UNITS

Shimano adopted an external cable system with the outer cables entering the levers at the top of the lever hoods. The brake cables pass under the bar tape. Shimano hoods are larger than Campagnolo and SRAM, and the whole brake lever moves in order to change gears.

CAMPAGNOLO ERGOPOWER

The obvious difference from Shimano controls is that Ergopower brake and gear cables are both taped under the handlebar tape. The main difference in function is that the brake lever is independent from the gear levers and the downshift is facilitated with a thumb button on the inside of the lever hood.

Campagnolo also developed their own take on index technology, and their Ergopower system was the first to have 10 gears.

SRAM

A late arrival to the road bike gear market, although SRAM already have a formidable reputation in the mountain bike market. Like Campagnolo, SRAM levers have an independent gear-shifting lever from the brake levers. Called Double Tap, their gearshift is done with just one lever: 'push' to shift up and 'tap' to shift down.

REPLACING INNER CABLES

Gear cables have a smaller nipple than brake cables and they're thinner (1.2mm). Shimano gear cables have a slightly bigger nipple than Campagnolo cables, so they're incompatible across systems. A squirt of Teflon lube on the cable is a good idea before installation, as it'll keep the cables loose and free-running.

To thread the cable through the lever mechanism, place the gear-shifter in the highest gear position. All systems require the lever and mech to be in top gear, so that the cable is slack and the nipple can be pushed out of the lever.

1 On Shimano and SRAM levers, you'll be able to see the white plastic cable-carrier. In this position the cable can be pushed through easily.

2 On Shimano levers, the cable simply passes straight through the lever and out of the cable port on the other side.

3 SRAM shifter cables are inserted at the inside, near the bottom of the lever housing, and exit the lever at the top.

5 New Campagnolo cables have a sharp, pointed end that makes threading the cable through the lever very easy.

4 On SRAM levers, as with Campagnolo, the outer cable can be taped and fitted into the handlebar before the tape is applied.

6 Pull the cable through until the nipple seats itself in the cable-carrier.

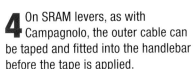

DOWN-TUBE GEARSHIFTS

Down-tube shifters were once the only gear-shifting choice. Nowadays they're rarely used – some climbers swap the front-mech shifter for a down-tube lever to save a few ounces, but the weight saved isn't really worth the effort. Down-tube levers mean that you have to take your hands off the handlebars to shift, but there's less cable and friction in the system, so they do last and provide very crisp shifts. Gear-adjusters are attached to most older frames designed for use with down-tube shifters. The gear-adjusters attach via a boss that is brazed to the frame. Campagnolo gear-adjusters rely on knurled-threaded adjusters with a spring under them to hold them in place – these do require cleaning and lubricating with a light oil to keep them easy to adjust. Shimano adjusters have a lever that can be turned to micro-adjust the gears as you ride. Seeing as most frames come without the standard-type bosses, these adjusters are becoming rare.

INSTALLING REAR MECHS

1 The rear mech needs to be installed onto the gear hanger. Check that the hanger is straight and that the threads are clean and uncrossed. If the hanger is bent or the mech cage is twisted, the system won't work. Use some grease or Ti-Prep lube on the threads to prevent the bolt from seizing.

2 The inner wire is clamped onto the rear mech by a washer. To see how this works, look for a channel moulded onto the body of the mech – the washer will be marked where the cable has been.

3 Screw the gear barrel adjuster fully in, so that there will be plenty of adjustment available when setting the cable tension. If all the cable outer sections are properly inserted and the gear-shifter is in the highest gear position, it should be possible to pull the cable tight enough with your hand. Pull the cable in the direction of the channel identified in step 2. Lock it off with the retaining screw.

4 The main difference between Campagnolo, Shimano and SRAM rear mechs is that they use a different sprung-pivot fixing bolt. This is at the bolt and gives you the advantage of a mechanism that moves as you shift between the chainrings.

5 Rear mechs work best with free-running jockey wheels. These can be replaced when the plastic wheels wear out. This improves shifting and helps keep the chain in contact with the sprockets on the cassette. To replace the jockey wheels, remove the pivot screws, paying attention to how it goes back together.

6 Strip and rebuild the jockey wheels after long periods of wet weather. The top jockey wheel may have a sealed bearing in it. It's worth stripping and reassembling both wheels. Clean them completely and reassemble using a Teflon lubricant.

7 Make sure that the jockey wheel is replaced so that it rotates in the right direction. There's usually an arrow on the plastic part of the wheel to help you do this. Once you've reassembled the cage, check that the top and bottom fixing screws are tight.

8 Lubricate the parallelogram mechanism with a light Teflon-based lube, especially the pivot points and internal springs.

9 Adjust the limit screw marked 'H' when the chain is in the smallest sprocket (highest gear). It's important that the chain can run smoothly over the sprocket and can't move any further down the block, trapping the chain between frame and cassette. It's a good idea to fit the chain now (see over).

10 Next, adjust the limit screw marked 'L' when the gear is in the largest sprocket. Double-check that the chain can reach this sprocket, and also that the chain can't jump over the top of the cassette and into the wheel. Also check that the mech can't hit the spokes of the wheel.

GEAR INDEXING – TUNING THE SHIFT

You need the back wheel off the ground, so use a workstand – leaving your hands free to pedal the bike and adjust the cable tension.

Start by running through each gear and listening for any noise as you change up the gears, going from the smallest cog to the largest one. Check how easily the chain skips the gears – if it struggles to make the next sprocket, the cable is too loose, so you'll need to tighten the cable by screwing the barrel adjuster anti-clockwise. Now change back down the gears (large to small cog) and check if there's a delay in the shift or if the chain stays stuck in one gear – if so, the cable is too tight and you'll need to loosen it by turning the adjuster clockwise.

Once the gears are adjusted and working smoothly, you need to stretch the cables. Place the gear in the highest position and identify the rear gear cable on the down tube. Tighten the cable clamp to ensure it won't pull through. Grab the inner cable firmly in the centre of the open run on the down tube. Pull the cable gently but firmly outwards a couple of times. This will seat the outer cables in place and bed the whole cable run into place. Then readjust as previous steps.

CHAINS: REPLACEMENT AND CARE

Chains are designed to wear out. They're incredibly efficient, but have to put up with a lot of abuse, and the constant twisting and shifting up and down the sprockets wears the average road bike chain out in a matter of months. Finer 10-speed chains also require a fair amount of careful cleaning and lubricating. (See page 47 for more on chain cleaning.)

There's also a variation in quality of chain. Plated chains are the best, as they're less likely to corrode and therefore last longer and shift better than a plain steel chain. Stainless steel and even titanium chains are also available – they may well last a little longer than plain steel chains but, as they're harder, they can wear aluminium chainrings if they aren't regularly cleaned and lubricated.

Replacing an old, worn-out chain usually requires replacing the cassette as well – as the chain stretches, it wears the cassette sprockets too, turning the whole drivetrain into scrap metal. This can be expensive, so using a cheap chain and replacing it often – rather than buying an expensive chain and waiting until it wears out the sprockets and chainring too – will turn out cheaper in the long run.

The chain is made up of side plates (external links) and internal links with rollers inside them. The rollers assist in the smooth running of the gearing and pedal action.

SHIMANO NINE- AND 10-SPEED CHAINS

1 Measure across 24 links of the chain – it should measure 12in. If it's more than that, the chain has stretched beyond a usable length. A chain in this state will start to wear other components and shifting will become increasingly erratic.

2 There are several chain-measuring devices, but the Park one pictured here is the best one on the market. Simply place the two pins into the links and turn the dial to ascertain how much stretch there is in the links. If the dial is in the red, the chain has stretched beyond serviceable life.

3 To check the chain and the chainrings for wear, put the chain on the biggest chainring and smallest cassette sprocket. If you can pull the chain off the chainring and it can clear the tip of one of the chainring teeth, or the chain moves excessively at the top and bottom of the chainring, this means the chain may need to be replaced.

NINE- AND 10-SPEED INSTALLATION

1 This darker-coloured, flat-ended pin marks the spot where the chain was first joined. If you're removing the chain to clean it and have a new link to rejoin the chain, find this link and break the chain exactly opposite it.

2 Remove the old chain and measure the new one next to it. Depending on the type of chain, you'll have to remove a certain number of links from one end. Leave the 'open' plates or external link end (seen here on the right) and remove links from the other end, leaving internal links ready for rejoining. This keeps the factory fitted end complete.

3 Thread the new chain through the rear mech jockey wheels and over the chainwheel. Don't put it back on the chainring until you've joined the chain, as the slack will make it easier to rejoin the two ends. The Shimano chain is joined with this special pin to make sure that the link is pushed in the correct way. Grease the pin so that it'll go in easily.

4 Push the link through using a quality Shimano chain-compatible chain-rivet tool. This Park tool has shaped jaws to prevent the side plates squeezing together. Keep the chain straight and turn the handle firmly and slowly to make sure that the pin goes through totally straight.

5 The Park chain tool is set up so that it stops once the link is in place (there's a circlip on the threaded shaft that prevents you going too far). There's a definite click as the pin passes through the link. When you reach this point, back off the handle and check that the pin is in place.

6 Although Shimano 10-speed chains use the same principles as a nine-speed chain, they're noticeably narrower and they use a specific 10-speed pin (rivet).

7 For 10-speed chains make sure that you use a genuine HG tool and that the pin is always pushed through from the outside. Check that the pin protrudes an equal distance either side of the plates.

8 When the Shimano (nine- or 10-speed) pin is through to the other side and the fatter part of the pin is equally spaced on either side of the link plates, snap off the guide with some pliers. Obviously, you need to do this before you check the gears are working.

9 Once the pin is in place there may be a little stiffness in the link, which may jump as you pedal the gears backwards. To remove a stiff link, first add some lube to it and push it into an inverted V-shape.

10 Then place your thumbs on the links to either side of this link. Grip the chain and very gently push the chain against itself. This very careful 'twisting' should free the link immediately.

SRAM CHAINS

SRAM chains started off life as Sachs/Sedis, two massive European chain manufacturers. Their expertise resulted in perhaps the best-shifting and most reliable chains on the market. SRAM now own these companies and they've created the easiest-to-install 10-speed system chain to date, and this is used in their Force and Rival Road race groupsets.

All nine- and 10-speed SRAM chains come with 'quick-release' links called Power Links. They can fix a chain without the need for tools and are really handy to use for emergencies – so carry one in your roadside tool kit. They're easy to install and save you messing about with chain tools every time you want to take a chain off.

To remove them, simply take the tension off the chain (I find it best to take the chain off the chainrings first) and push the links against each other and your hands towards one another at the same time. It takes practice, but is a great way to remove your chain for washing. Ten-speed Power Links can't be removed and a new link has to be used once the chain has been broken.

FITTING SRAM 10-SPEED CHAINS

1 To get the correct chain length, measure the chain so that it's tight when placed from biggest sprocket to biggest chainring, bypassing the rear mech (it's easiest to do this before the rear mech is attached).

2 Then add two links to this length. Bear in mind that fitting Power Links requires removing the side plates from both ends of the chain so they join the chain between two rollers.

3 Then install the rear mech and thread the chain though the jockey wheels over the chainrings and through the front mech, join the two open ends of chain with the Power Link and slot the pins into place – they'll sit halfway, not quite bedded into the closed position.

4 Use the crank arm and brace the rear wheel so that you can 'snap' the Power Link into place – it'll seat into place, and the main advantage is that no tools are required and it's impossible to get a stiff link.

CHAIN TIPS

1 For the best results, replace your chain every 2,000–3,000km (1,250–1,850mi). This will prevent wear to the cassette sprockets, chainrings and mechs.

2 Swap steel rings for aluminium ones and replace them at least every one to two years. Make sure that you use 10-speed compatible chainrings and mechs, as they too are designed to work only with narrow chains.

3 Buy a chain bath and clean your chain once a week. (See page 46 for more on chain cleaning.)

4 Degrease and thoroughly clean a new chain before using it. They're packed in grease for storage to stop them from rusting, but this just attracts dirt. Run the chain through a chain bath and re-lubricate with a quality chain lube. This will keep your new chain clean for longer.

5 A chain 'jumps' when there's something worn in the drivetrain. Usually, if you fit a new chain it'll skip over the cassette sprockets in some ratios, which means that the cassette needs replacing too. However, there may be a stiff link – see opposite for how to remedy this.

6 If you want to experiment with chain lengths, do so with an old chain. You can then run through the gears and decide on the final length before you cut a new one and measure it next to the old one.

5 Once the Power Link is in place, you'll have to break the chain next time opposite this link and use a new Power Link each time you rejoin the chain. SRAM chains are supplied with spare Power Links.

CAMPAGNOLO CHAINS

Campagnolo pioneered the 10-speed chain and shifting system in 1999. The chain has been through several changes over the past few years and the result is the Campagnolo Record Ultra Narrow chain. This does require very careful installation, as the pins and links are very delicate when installed incorrectly. However, it's simple enough if you use the right tools and follow the recommended methods.

1 The 10-speed Campagnolo chain has a serial number stamped on the external link. This is very important, as it denotes the link that needs to be left untampered with. The external links are designed specifically to face a certain way to accept the countersunk pin that joins the two ends of chain together.

2 A Campagnolo 10-speed HD chain-pin has a detachable guide pin and a hollow rivet – this guide pin simply slots into the rivet and can be taken out once the chain has been joined.

3 The HD pin is always placed on the inside of the drivetrain, so as to be pushed outwards of the bike (for the reason explained in step 1).

4 Measure the chain in the small sprocket and inner chain wheel. When the chain ends are pulled together you're looking for a gap of around 15mm between the chainline along the bottom and the top of the lower jockey wheel.

5 The rear mech should just take up the slack in the chain, and the chain should run clear of the jockey wheel cage guides (the tab at the rear of this cage).

6 Place the chain on the big ring and link up the chain with the connecting pin. Join the chain under the chainring from the inside out – double-check that you have the stamped external plate on the outside before you do this.

7 The Campagnolo chain tool has a locking pin that pushes across the internal and external links to ensure that the chain is held tightly and the links are perfectly aligned.

8 It may appear over-complicated, but special 'HD Link' rejoining links are required if the chain is broken and needs to be rejoined. Measure the same length of links and remove the same amount from the chain opposite the first join. This can then be installed with two HD pins.

FRONT MECH (DERAILLEUR)

As with rear mechs, Shimano have perfected this mechanism to be indexed, so now one click at the lever allows for one chainring shift at the cranks. At least, that's the theory. Setting up and using the front mech properly takes time and practice. It's a very dynamic mechanism, so it does require patience to get it perfect. Height, angle and throw are all influencing factors.

The plates are shaped so that they won't rub on the chain when they're set correctly, and so that they can pick up the chain and carry it to the next chainring. For many mechanics, the front mech is often their biggest headache.

There are two types of fitting for the front mech. Braze-on will fit a frame with a mech hanger already attached to it, while band-on have the clamp as a part of the mechanism. Braze-on is preferred these days, as retro-fitting bands are available to attach the mech too.

INSTALLING AND ADJUSTING THE FRONT MECH

1 Angle the mech so that it's exactly parallel with the big chainring. If you can't get the mech into this position, you may have problems with the chainline and, if so, you may need a different length bottom bracket.

2 If the angle is slightly out, the shifting will be sloppy, so make sure you set the angle carefully. If it's angled too far outwards, it'll foul the crank when the pedals are turned. A good chainline is imperative, so make sure that the chain can access all of the rear sprockets when in the inner chainring. You can also see here that the ideal mech position is parallel with the outer (big) chainring.

3 The distance between the outside mech plate and the teeth of the chainring should be no more than 2–3mm. This will ensure that the mech is correctly positioned to cope with the difference in size of the inner and big rings.

4 This set-up is with smaller chainrings (Compact drive), and although it'll probably work OK, the gap at the bottom of the cage is much greater than at the top, the result being a sloppy shift. If you're using Compact cranks, consider a Compact-specific front mech.

CAUSES OF FRONT MECH RUBBING

- The cable is too tight or too loose.

- The limit screws are incorrectly adjusted.

- The angle of the mech to the chainrings is wrong.

- The chainline is incorrect (which requires closer attention to the bottom bracket).

5 This SRAM front mech is positioned perfectly for tight and crisp changes – check that the outside plate clears all the teeth, though 3mm will allow for the chain pick-up and will happily clear the teeth of the chainrings.

6 Next, attach the gear cable. Make sure that the gear-shifter is in its lowest position so that the cable is at its slackest and the front mech is over the inner ring. Pull the cable through the clamp firmly. Trap the cable in the clamp and check that it's in the right place, as this can affect the shift. Now, adjust the low-limit stop screw.

7 Adjust the limit screw marked 'L' first. Place the rear mech in the biggest sprocket and the front onto the smallest, as this is the furthest the chain will travel. Then set the front mech so it only just clears the inside of the plate without rubbing.

8 Now, adjust the limit screw marked 'H'. Put the chain onto the big chainring (this may over-shift at first) and work the rear mech through all the gears. You'll notice that the chain changes angle considerably, but it'll cope with most of the gears on this chainring. Set the limit screw so that it just clears the chain in the smallest rear sprocket.

CAUSES OF UNSHIPPING A CHAIN

- The low adjust is set incorrectly, so you'll have to push the mech further out with the limit screw.

- The chain is jumping over the top of the big chainring, so you'll need to push the mech further in with the limit screw.

- The distance between the mech plates and the chainring is too great or the angle is badly adjusted.

CAMPAGNOLO LIMIT SCREWS

1 The top limit screw adjusts the throw of the chain to the inner chainring.

2 And the bottom one adjusts the throw to the big chain ring.

11-SPEED

CAMPAGNOLO 11

Chances are if you buy a new bike with Campagnolo Record or Chorus groupset on it the bike will now have 11-speed gearing. That's 22 gears. We've come a long way from the ten-speed racer.

Campagnolo introduced 11-speed gears in 2008, much fuss was made about the extra sprocket, but the truth is you won't really notice the benefits (over 9 or 10-speed). There are engineering reasons for this – less strain on certain gear ratios and a slightly closer ratio gear (a 11-23 cassette is almost one tooth per sprocket). Combined with a compact crankset with 34-50 or 36-52 ratio chainwheels and you will have a combination able to climb any mountain.

Campagnolo cassettes for 11 speed are only compatible with 11-speed chains and you'll need a special chain tool, but other than that the principles of set-up are exactly the same as 10 speed. Campagnolo's ratios for 11-speed cassettes are: 11-23, 11-25, 12-25, 12-27 and 12-29.

The good news is you can use your old Campagnolo compatible 10 or 9-speed wheels as all new Campagnolo 11-speed set ups (including EPS) use the same cassette carriers as 9 and 10 speed so the cassette and hub servicing information (on previous pages) will still apply.

SHIMANO 11-SPEED

At the time of going to press on this book, Shimano had just launched their Dura Ace 9000 11-speed groupset. So now, Shimano and Campagnolo are level pegging in terms of sprockets and electronic gear shifting.

The big news with this is there is now just one crankset that covers a multitude of chainring sizes, so if you want to have a race bike and one that's happy plodding up steep mountains too, then Shimano have that covered. The new design is a four-arm spider rather than a five arm and this not only allows a solution to the compatibility headaches – it's also lighter and just as stiff as previous versions. So you can have 52-36T and 52-38T chainsets for those who want some lower gears without sacrificing the higher. They also cover the more traditional ratios of: 50-34T, 53-39T, 54-42T and 55-42T.

The downside of Shimano's new group is that the hub cassette carrier is a new design, so your old wheels will not work with the new 11-speed cassettes.

SHIMANO AND CAMPAGNOLO NOW BOTH HAVE ELECTRONIC 11-SPEED GEAR SYSTEMS AVAILABLE. REMARKABLY EFFICIENT, THE BATTERIES LAST A FEW THOUSAND KILOMETRES ON EACH CHARGE

ELECTRONIC GROUPSETS – CAMPAGNOLO EPS AND SHIMANO Di2

Shimano's Di2 Electronic shifting groupset has been in action for a few seasons now and slowly is becoming more popular for consumers. All the set-up principles for frames are the same as cable gears, the only difference is the cable set up, and it needs a battery. Adjustment is done electronically too, so although it may seem a bit space age and Formula 1, electronic gears are actually easier to maintain than their cabled counterparts. Professional riders have embraced the new Di2 group, however there are still some races where riders prefer to use cable gears.

Electronic Power Shifting (EPS) was Campagnolo's first retail attempt at electric gears, but their EPS group is now established with many professional race teams. Both Shimano and Campagnolo have similar attributes from the point of view of function.

Obviously for some the idea of having a completely new frame (with internal cable routing) isn't a great one and retro-fitting either Di2 or EPS to a standard cable-fitted frame is messy and compromised. If you are a racer or money is no object then it's worthwhile for the added performance benefit – but it's so slight most riders will realise that the extra cost, for now, isn't really worth it.

CABLE ROUTING ON FRAMES IS NOW BEST AS INTEGRATED INTO THE FRAME TUBES. CABLE ROUTING IS LESS OF AN ISSUE WITH ELECTRONIC SYSTEMS, ONCE IT'S IN PLACE YOU CAN PRETTY MUCH FORGET ABOUT IT

GEAR LIMIT SCREW ADJUSTMENT IS DONE AS ON CABLE GEAR SYSTEMS, SHIMANO HAS ALLEN KEY SCREWS ACCESSED FROM THE REAR

GEAR INDEXING ADJUSTMENT ON SHIMANO SYSTEMS IS DONE WITH THIS HANDY BUTTON UNIT PLACED ON THE CABLES UNDER THE HANDLEBARS. ONCE PRESSED, THE ADJUSTMENT IS DONE AUTOMATICALLY

CABLE ROUTING ON CAMPAGNOLO EPS SYSTEMS IS ALMOST IDENTICAL TO SHIMANO ALTHOUGH THE ADJUSTMENT BUTTON IS IN THE LEVER

THE SHIMANO DI2 FRONT DERAILLEUR IS SELF ADJUSTING AND SET UP IS IDENTICAL TO CABLE SYSTEMS. SEE PAGE 130

07

BRAKES AND CABLES

Road bike brake callipers have improved enormously over the past decade. Dual-pivot brakes are designed to allow increased efficiency at the wheel and so that the rider's input at the lever is maximised at the rim. In simple terms, a series of linked levers over two pivots apply greater braking pressure.

Brakes need good braking surfaces and true wheels to work properly. Buckled wheels and damaged old rims in poor condition are not only unsafe but will also hinder your riding enjoyment. Braking should be easy and effortless, so if you are putting more effort into 'stopping' than you are into 'going', you should pay some careful attention to your brakes and ensure that your wheels are in good order too.

Until disc brakes come to road bikes, road bike brakes will rely on simple cable-activated callipers, as this is the lightest and easiest solution. Campagnolo's Record brakes perform the best in my opinion, especially since they have added a lighter and less grabby 'differential' single-pivot rear brake system, as most of your braking is done on the front wheel and a 'weaker' rear brake allows you to adopt more gradual stopping.

GENERAL BRAKE ADJUSTMENTS

RELEASING BRAKES

All road brakes have a facility that allows you to back off the brakes in order to be able to remove the wheels – the loosening of the brake calliper allows the tyre to pass easily through the brake pads (see removing wheels on page 40).

Campagnolo have placed the QR on the brake lever.

Shimano brakes use a small lever on the brake itself, next to the fixing bolts.

1 On Campagnolo brakes, the small aluminium button on the inside of the lever needs to be depressed before the wheels can be removed.

2 Once released, this will back off the levers and release the pads away from the wheel rim. Remember to return the lever button before riding.

3 On Shimano brakes, the QR lever is on the callipers. This is the lever in the 'open' position.

4 And this is the QR in the 'closed', ready-to-ride position.

FIXING THE CALLIPERS TO THE BIKE

1 Rear brake callipers have a shorter fixing bolt and nut than front brakes. The brake bridge is drilled to take the recessed bolt shown here.

2 Fit a star washer in between the brake and the frame to secure the calliper and prevent the brake from loosening under normal conditions.

BRAKE BITE?

Over-slack cables and extra movement at the lever may mean that the pads have started to wear. You can adjust cable tension 'on the fly' using the adjusters on the brakes.

3 Brake callipers attach to the frame and fork with Allen key nuts. They have a variety of lengths to fit different fork crowns. Fatter fork crowns and wider brake bridges need longer fixing nuts. Brakes have to have at least 1cm of thread held by the nut for safety's sake.

4 Install the wheels and tighten the calliper fixing bolts while squeezing the pads onto the rim. This will roughly centre the brake over the rims and allow you to install the cables and adjust the brake pads.

5 Centring the brakes makes the most of the braking efficiency and prevents the pads from rubbing on the rim. The brakes will also respond faster and feel better at the lever when accurately centred.

6 Shimano brakes can be centred without disturbing the brake fixing bolt. The adjustment screw on the top of the brake allows for fine tuning and perfect alignment.

7 Campagnolo calliper springs can be adjusted for tension too, which just allows for fine tuning the feel at the lever for personal preference rather than improving brake function.

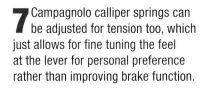

8 SRAM callipers use a smaller 10mm spanner to centre the brake pads over the rim – when using a spanner like this always double-check that the fixing bolt is still tight in the frame/fork after adjusting.

BRAKE REACH ADJUSTMENT TIPS

1   Experiment with the position of the levers on the bars (see page 153).

2   Use a round, shallow drop bar that allows you to get closer to the lever.

3   Shimano offer an after-market converter that can bring the STI lever closer to the bars.

4   Don't run the brake cables too tight, as some slack in the braking system will actually allow your hands to wrap around the lever more.

BRAKE PAD ALIGNMENT

The key to brake pad alignment is to have a perfectly central brake calliper and to line the pads up perfectly to the rim, so as to prevent the pad from rubbing against the tyre and to prevent uneven wear to the surface of the pad.

Shimano brake systems have a lot of brute force available and are perhaps the easiest to set up.

1 Campagnolo's pad system features a domed washer, which allows you to toe-in the pad and adjust the angle of the pad in relation to the rim.

2 Toe-in is a useful feature to any rim-braked system, as it prevents the brakes from squealing and improves performance. The pad has to hit the rim at the front of the block first.

3 Pad alignment is equally important in relation to the braking surface and to make sure that the pad clears the tyres. Friction on the tyre can cause damage to the sidewalls.

4 Campagnolo's latest Record Skelton callipers now use Torq-headed nuts on their brake fittings.

5 SRAM adopt a similar system to both Campagnolo and Shimano. The adjustment of the pads is similar to Campagnolo's and the cartridge pad system more like Shimano's.

BRAKE TIPS

1 Overlong cable outers will usually add friction and absorb braking power, so keep the cable lengths to a minimum without sacrificing movement in the handlebars.

2 Oil cable inner wires and check for kinks and fraying in the cable runs. Replace the outers if they split.

3 Clean rims will make a huge difference to brake performance. Use solvent-based disc-brake cleaner to clean your rims and regularly remove all the grime that builds up, as brake dust will just act as an abrasive and wear down both the rim and the pads.

4 Brake squealing is caused by vibration. As the pad hits the rim, it applies friction to slow the wheel down. The result of this friction is vibration and a build-up of heat. This wears down the brake pads and can also create a hell of a racket. Toe in the pads and you'll alleviate the problem. However, if this still doesn't work there may be excessive play in the brake assembly and it may need to be replaced.

5 Brake pads wear fairly evenly and slowly in the dry. However, in the wet you can wear through a set in a matter of hours, especially in the mountains.

FITTING CARTRIDGE BRAKE PADS

Cartridge brake shoes are a better option than totally replaceable brake pads. They are stronger (stiffer) than all-rubber replaceable pads and they can stay in place, and therefore don't need to be adjusted after the pads have been replaced.

Over-slack cables and extra movement at the lever may mean that the pads have started to wear. You can adjust cable tension 'on the fly' using the adjusters on the brakes.

Long-term adjustment of the slack in a cable system is best done by pulling the cable through at the brake cable fastening bolt on the calliper, and all brake pads have a wear-line indicator that should be checked regularly, especially after long periods of wet-weather riding.

1 Campagnolo pads require a very small amount of light grease or Vaseline smeared into the cartridge slot to help the pads slide into place.

2 Position the opening and the pad in the slot. There is a left and right pad and a left- and right-facing cartridge, so before you start make sure that you have the pads and cartridges aligned correctly.

3 Push the brake pad into place. This may require a fair bit of force as the pads are supposed to be a tight fit. The open end of the cartridge should always face back so the rotation of the wheel will force the pad against the closed end's shoulder – if orientated incorrectly, the pads can be forced out of the cartridge.

4 Shimano pads have a screw that retains the pad in the cartridge.

CARBON FIBRE RIMS

Carbon fibre rim-braking can be problematic – because of its grippy, uneven surface texture, it can't offer the same predictable braking that a machined-smooth aluminium rim can.

The reputation is basically 'all or nothing' and, in the wet, it's often nothing. Do not use standard rubber compound brake pads, as they will grab at the rims, set up dangerous vibrations and even lock the wheels completely.

You should always look to use the brand of pad that the wheel manufacturer recommends. Cork compounds from Zipp, Shimano and Swissstop can improve braking. Although never as good as aluminium rims, when fitted with the correct pads they can at least provide predictable and safe stopping.

5 They will slide in and out very easily once this screw is loosened.

CABLE REPLACEMENT

You should check for cable trouble on a regular basis, and always take care of your cables when releasing the brakes to remove the wheels and packing the bike for travel.

Damaged cables and water inside the cable outers will slow your braking down considerably. It's sometimes hard to tell when the inner wire is kinked, but a sloppy or stiff feeling in the lever action is a dead giveaway. Replacing the cable run is the best way to solve this, but stripping out the inner and using a quality spray lube can be a short-term fix.

It's pretty rare for a brake cable to fray dangerously, but it's worth checking the inner cable, especially if the brakes are feeling stiffer than usual.

Is there a notchy brake feel? This can also signify that the brake cables have been badly installed, as this added friction is usually caused by the inner cable rubbing on either a burr at the end of the outer cable or a damaged frame cable stop. It's also rare for cables to snap, but they can fray at the clamp bolts, which can make future adjustment difficult.

A slack feeling at the lever with a slow lever return may also mean that the cables need replacing. With cheaper brakes this may also signify the brake springs and pivots have seized.

1 All systems require the cable outer to enter the rear of the brake lever. Make sure that the cable has been neatly cut and there are no sharp edges on the inside.

2 Shimano STI lever housings bury the cable nipple retainer deep inside the lever housing. Flick the lever to one side to allow the lever to fall further forwards and allow easy access.

3 Once the inner cable is in place the grommet can be returned to its position in the lever housing.

4 Campagnolo cables feature a sharp uncut end that makes it very easy to thread the inner wire through the lever.

5 SRAM brake cabling is very similar to Campagnolo's (although it is slightly easier to install).

6 Greasing the brake cable nipple will prevent friction and stop any noises developing as the levers are applied, and it prevents wear and tear on the cable around the nipple too.

7 Cables should be measured (it's easiest to use the old cables as a template) and cut using a quality cable cutter. Make sure that the ends of the cable are flat – they can be tidied up with a metal file – and that the inner nylon part is open at the ends.

9 The rear brake cable must be precision-cut so that the curve of the cable is unhindered and smooth. Overlong cables flap about and create friction. However, short cables will pull on the callipers and potentially de-centralise them over the rims.

11 Thread the inner cable through the fixing bolt and pull the callipers together onto the rim. Fasten the inner cable into the calliper using a 5mm Allen key. Leave 20-30mm of cable to allow for further adjustment, and cut the cable with a sharp cable cutter.

8 Unlike gear cables, it is only necessary to add a ferrule where the cable will contact the frame stops. The V-brake noodle has its own built-in ferrule. New brake cables usually have a factory fitted ferrule on one end – I always start with this one at the lever adjuster.

10 Cable doughnuts are used to prevent the cable slapping on the top tube and wearing out the paintwork (the noise of flapping cables is also highly annoying).

12 Lastly, add a cable-end cap to prevent the cable from fraying. This will prevent injury (the ends can be very sharp) and enable you to make further adjustments to the brakes.

08

CONTACT POINTS

The contact points on a bicycle are: the saddle; the handlebars; and the pedals. These are all very simple parts, so usually the ones that get the least attention and servicing. But looking after them is essential for rider comfort and safety and as such they should never be neglected.

Professional bike riders are often obsessive about their favourite brand of saddle and preferred handlebar shape and when you are spending as long as they do on a bike that's more than reasonable. The point of contact that requires the most mechanical attention is the pedals and these need regular care as do the cleats and the shoes. As a group the contact points are the least complicated components on the bike, but the ones that you are in constant touch with. Look after them.

SEAT POSTS AND SADDLES

SEAT POSTS
MATERIALS
Seat posts are usually made out of aluminium. The best pins are made from butted Easton EA 70 tubing, 7075-T6 or 6061-T6.

Cro-Mo steel posts are strong and therefore great for cyclo-cross and track, but they do weigh a bit more. They're best suited to riders who are better on the flat than they are in the mountains!

Titanium is an excellent seat post material, as it has inherent flex and is super-strong. Titanium or steel are also better if you have a compact frame and want to use an extra-long post (more than 300mm).

Carbon fibre shafts are now becoming increasingly popular, but extreme care must be taken with carbon posts, especially after crashes and prolonged periods of wet weather.

(See page 18 for more on carbon fibre.)

FAILURES
The worst-case scenario is a snap, but this will usually be the result of riding around on a bent or damaged post for a while and thus placing too much stress on the material – the constant bending results in a fatigue fracture. It's usually only an issue on compact frames where there's much more than 250mm showing from the frame. You can easily check for a bend by placing a straight edge (ruler) next to it and eyeing it up front and back and side-to-side. Do this regularly, especially after a crash.

The clamp can break in various places – the yokes (the two halves that clamp the saddle rails together) can snap, or the serrations that hold the cradle can wear smooth and leave you with your saddle pointing skywards. I've found that some cheap, bonded clamps (where the clamp is glued and push-fitted into the shaft) are also prone to failure – this is not normally dangerous, but is very annoying. Good quality posts are less likely to fail, and regular cleaning and checking will prevent nasty accidents.

The saddle clamp is in two halves – one holds the saddle to the post and the other adjusts the angle of the saddle.

The shaft of an aluminium seat post should always be smeared with anti-seize grease before inserting it into the seat tube. It should slide in without any pressure being applied and there shouldn't be any side-to-side movement before the clamp bolt is tightened. The anti-seize grease will also prevent the different materials from seizing together. When setting your saddle height, never go beyond the minimum insert mark usually etched into the post (see 'Length', below). If you have to, the chances are that the post is too short or your bike is too small!

LENGTH
Seat posts come in several lengths, with 250mm and 300mm being the most common in road bikes. As I've said, you need a pin that leaves plenty of material in the frame – pins usually have a line to indicate the minimum insertion level ('Min. Insertion') or maximum height ('Max. Ht.'). Don't exceed this – it not only protects the seat post, but also prevents placing excess strain on the top of the frame's seat tube/clamp area, which can easily be distorted by the extra leverage on the little bit left in the frame.

SIZE (DIAMETER)
This depends on the material that the frame is made of. Steel and standard aluminium frames usually come in 26.4–27.2mm sizes, but some specialist frames can be as little as 25mm and as much as 32.7mm. Getting the recommended size for your frame is essential, as even 0.2mm either way can make a difference to the correct fit. If it's too big, it can swell the seat tube and make it difficult to fit or remove – if it's too small, it can move about, damaging the collar and distorting the top of the seat tube.

FITTING SADDLES
There are several types of seat post cradle and most good-quality posts have a one-bolt fixing. This means that the cradle will be removable and easy to rebuild. Saddles now have cut-away sides and this makes it much easier to access under the rails and fit the top cradle.

Seat posts with dual bolts are very secure but harder to adjust. I like these because they tend to stay put and are less likely to make a noise or rattle loose like some single-bolt seat posts can.

1 To adjust the saddle angle, loosen the post at the back bolt. Then the front bolt (here with a knurled nut so it can be done by hand) can either be tightened to point the nose of the saddle downwards, or loosened to point the nose up.

2 Use a Bondhus round-headed Allen key to access the bolt to the rear of the post, which requires tightening at an angle – this prevents scratching the post and allows a full rotation of the bolt.

3 If the seat post clamp has serrations, make sure that these are clean and thoroughly degreased. Here, the black oxide indicates an area of friction where the cradle has been ridden loose and has started to wear.

4 Clean the insides of the clamp. Dry off and wipe with a light oil. Don't use grease on the saddle clamping area.

5 Single-clamp seat post bolts need lubricating around the wedges and spacers – again, use a light oil.

6 The threads also benefit from some lubrication, although make sure that any excess lube (grease can be used here) is cleaned off, as the seat post is in direct line of the rear wheel and all the road grime is attracted to the clamp area.

7 Remove and clean carbon fibre posts regularly. Use a bike polish that can buff the post to a shine.

8 Clean the inside of the seat tube. You mustn't grease carbon posts – so, if the frame is tight fitting or in poor internal condition, you may well be better off with an aluminium post. If you must fit a carbon post, seat tubes can be reamed out to clean up the insides and prepare them.

9 Make sure that there are no sharp edges and burrs inside the seat tube, and that the seat post collar is undone, before trying to insert the carbon post. Scratches in the surface of the lacquer (like these shown here) are OK as long as they're below the insertion point – deep scratches and gouges are not OK. Any damage to the surface layer of carbon means that the post should be replaced immediately.

10 If you're using a carbon post, fit a saddle collar like this Campagnolo one. This prevents the collar from binding up around the back of the seat tube slot and damaging the post. If you have a standard seat collar, you can turn the collar around so that the slots are opposite one another. Damage in this area can be catastrophic, so be careful.

11 Only tighten to manufacturers' recommended torque settings. If your post still slips, don't keep tightening it – the chances are that you need a different-diameter post or your frame needs attention. Over-tightening carbon posts can crush the post's tube, so be careful. If you have to tighten up harder, change for an aluminium or titanium post.

NOISES

The seatpost can be a source of annoying creaks and squeaks. Usually, a thorough clean and rebuild of the clamp will eradicate the creaks. Remember to check the saddle rails too, especially where they join the underside of the saddle. A squirt of lube into the ends of the rails can be enough to keep friction at bay. Clean the underside of your saddle regularly, as it does get the worst of the wet weather.

HANDLEBAR SET-UP

POSITION

There's a simple test for checking your handlebar position (see also 'bike set-up' on pages 34-35) – take a look at your handlebar tape. Where is it most worn? On the tops? Behind the brake levers? Or on the drops?

Many riders hardly ever use the drop part of their bars, usually because they're too low and too far away to be used comfortably. Handlebar choice can play a great part in getting comfortable, so select the bar that has the right reach, width and drop, as riders generally use bars that are too big in all these dimensions.

BAR MEASUREMENT

Most manufacturers state the bar's measurement from centre to centre. Standard road bars are 42cm, and these will be fine for almost everyone, but some women and younger riders may opt for smaller bars with less reach. Bars are available in 38cm to 48cm sizes, and some companies offer other designs that are even wider. It's best to buy handlebars at the width of your shoulders. The wider the bar, the more control you'll

have over the steering, hence cyclo-cross riders often go a size up – they can also get more leverage out of a wider bar. But a wider bar takes more effort, as your arms are best used parallel, so narrow bars are more efficient for sprinting and climbing.

ROUND BARS

Once upon a time, all bars were round. Thankfully, there are a few companies that still make round handlebars. They usually come in shallow- and deep-drop form. The former are better for riders with smaller hands, and the latter for sprinters and track riders.

TRACK BARS

Steel bars are for sprinters. They're heavy but offer unparalleled strength and stiffness, which is essential for getting the power down. They tend to have a very deep drop, so aren't really suited to endurance track riders, who may prefer to fit the same bar as they use on the road. When setting up a track bike, bear in mind that your 'cruising' on the lever hood position will shift slightly. Also, narrower bars are sometimes the preferred choice for squeezing through gaps and keeping your arms narrow.

ERGO BARS

Most bar manufacturers offer a variety of handlebar shapes. These are intended to offer more comfortable hand positions and ergonomic comfort than round bars – however, if set up incorrectly they can provide the exact opposite. Generally, Ergo bars offer a flatter section just behind the brake levers, intended for sprinting and descending in comfort. Set this angle to suit you before you mount the brake lever, as it's important to have this position right before you worry about how the levers fit. Getting the right bar can take time, so spending hundreds of pounds on bars is never a great idea – this is partly because they mightn't suit you, but also because if you crash they can be easily ruined. My advice is to buy (cheaper) aluminium bars and try several different makes out until you know exactly what suits you – the 'ergonomics' differ quite a lot.

1 Handlebars should be positioned in the stem carefully – aim to keep them as scratch-free as possible. When installing them, take care not to twist them in the stem too much, as this can scratch the surface of the bar, which creates a stress riser and can fail at a later date.

2 There's usually a mark or series of marks on the bar where the centre section is. This will also give you an idea of the preferred angle of the bar. Line this up with the front cap of the stem.

3 The flat ends of the bar should be at the bottom of the bend, either parallel with the stem or the floor. Round bars usually need the flat part pointing towards the axle of the rear hub. When fitting new bars, establish the right riding angles, and that the drop position is feeling natural and comfortable, before you start to add the brake levers.

4 To fit the levers, first remove the clip from the rear of the lever – don't try to push the lever on with the clip still attached, as it'll only scratch the surface of the bar (especially important with carbon bars).

5 Slide the clip into position – they're a snug fit so should hold their position OK. Some bars have a rough section behind the bar at the lever position to add grip and indicate the point to position the lever.

6 All makes of lever (pictured is Shimano) have a recessed 5mm Allen nut inside the lever housing, which attaches to the bolt trapped in the lever clip. It helps to pull the rubber hood back a little to locate the lever housing over the bolt.

7 On Shimano this can be accessed via a channel on the outside of the lever hood.

8 SRAM and Campagnolo levers require the lever hood to be rolled forwards (be careful not to rip the hood as you pull it over the thumb lever on Campagnolo levers). Use a T-bar Allen key to access the nut on these types.

9 Line the tip of the brake lever up with the base of the bar (flat section) – use a ruler and get this approximate before trying different hand positions to get the feel right.

10 The controls can be positioned parallel to the ground – use a ruler to line them up with the flat top section of the bar. Don't over-tighten them, as the levers' clips can easily break. Levers can also bend if they're not allowed to move a little in the event of a crash.

HANDLEBAR SET-UP TIPS

1   Creaking bars? Most noises from handlebars can easily be eliminated by stripping the bar from the stem, cleaning it with parts cleaner and rebuilding the stem with fresh grease or copper slip on the fixing bolts. Take the stem off, check the fork steerer and clean it too.

2   Replace bars after bad crashes and after a couple of years' heavy use. Failure is rare, but you won't get a great deal of warning before they go – so treat them with respect. Interchange different sets of bars on a regular basis, as they're more likely to fail after prolonged usage.

3   Lever position can take a while to get spot-on – many riders are always tweaking their bars and lever position. The 'correct' riding position is with the hands placed naturally on the lever hoods – if you find them too hard to reach, it may be that the levers need moving towards you or that the stem is too long, or even that the bike is too long (see more on sizing on page 34).

4   With the hands wrapped around the lever hoods it's easy to change gear and brake without too much effort. If you have to remove your hands from the tops of the bars and move them forwards to brake or shift, there's something wrong with your bar and lever set-up. It shouldn't require you to move much at all, and above all it should be comfortable.

5   It's essential that you can comfortably reach the brake levers, wrapping your fingers around the lever to get full leverage. Ergo bars don't always allow this, especially for riders with smaller hands.

HANDLEBAR TAPE

There are several ways to apply handlebar tape. Every mechanic will have their personal approach, so none can be described as the textbook method. Clean bar tape gives your bike a lift and it's best done after a good (or stripdown) service. So here's one way of doing it.

Pro riders and their mechanics can be absolutely obsessed with clean, smooth tape and some track riders have been known to have their tape redone even in the moments before the start of a big race if there is a patch that's not up to standard.

Like any finishing touch, it's all down to taking your time and being prepared, choosing the right tape and making sure it's the last job you do on the bike. Wash your hands and have everything at hand, as you do need to have both hands free to do this job properly.

Getting the tape smooth is the priority, but you want to make sure there are no bits uncovered. Overlap the tape by a third with each wrap – this will vary according to where you are on the bend or flat section, but always check that the bit you are covering up hasn't got creased underneath. There is nothing more distracting than a lump under the bar tape.

Judging the 'pull' on the end of the tape comes down to experience, and the tension should be increased a little if the sticky backing is no good. A good bar wrap needs to be tightly

TOOLS REQUIRED

- **Electrical Insulating tape**
- **Scissors**
- **Allen keys (5mm T-Bar is useful for brake levers)**

wound – however, pull too hard and you risk ripping the fabric.

1 First, strip off any of the old tape and any tape or debris stuck to the bars. Clean the surface of the bars, as the sweat penetrates the tape and can make the bars a bit greasy and unpleasant. Use an alcohol-based cleaner or citrus degreaser. Clean off any residue and dry off completely. Fix the levers in place (see previous pages for details).

2 Pull the rubber lever hoods away from the bars and fold them inside out (be careful as you can rip them). This allows clear access behind and means that the underside can be wrapped easily.

3 Then tape the control cables in place with electrical insulating tape (make sure that the controls are correctly aligned first). Unsecured cables will help unravel the tape, and spend some time making sure that they are long enough and don't need replacing.

4 Some mechanics wrap the whole top section of bar so that the cables don't 'drift' under the tape – it's essential to secure the cables this way under the tape so they will be out of the way when you start applying the top layer of tape.

5 Campagnolo Ergopower levers require both gear and brake cables to be wrapped under the tape. Most handlebars have a groove rolled into the section so the cable can recess slightly and remain comfortable to hold.

6 There are grooves at the front for brake cables and at the rear for gear cables. If there is a separate channel for gear and brake cables and you are using Shimano levers, you can add a filling section (use a cut strip of the old bar tape) into the rear channel so that the tape will be smooth and round on the back when wrapped up.

7 Bar tape usually comes with an extra short section to be curled around the back of the brake lever clasp and fittings. Cut this so that it can cover the back of the bar around the brake lever. (On Campagnolo Ergo levers this may need to be angled slightly, as the lever body is a little longer than Shimano.)

8 Decent cork tape is sticky backed so it stays in place, and this may be protected with paper backing. Peel a little of the backing off (not all of it at once, as you may stick it to itself, a bike part, the cat, etc). Start at the open end of the bar with the end of the tape at the underside of the bar and work from the inside out, and leave three-quarters of the width of the tape to overlap the end of the bar.

9 Continue to wrap the tape around, angling it so that the overlap will cover the next wrap of tape, especially around the bend, until you get two turns from the lever. Judge how many turns it will take to reach the lever and cover the bar and the levers without a gap, and adjust the overlap slightly to get to this point.

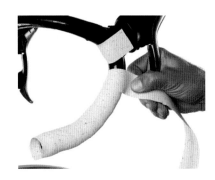

10 If you approach the lever at the right angle, you can take the tape around the back of the lever and over the top of it once, which should cover the section and both sides of the lever in one turn. This can be influenced by the shape of the bar and the position of the levers.

11 Here we have gone around the back and over the top of the lever, but this may mean you have to give it a couple of goes to get it right. Try repositioning the short bit underneath so that it helps cover the bits the tape misses.

12 The section on the top of the bar, just behind the brake lever, is the section that gets the most wear, so pay careful attention to getting the overlap here consistent. Any gaps, 'under-lapped' bits or creases under the tape here will cause you all sorts of bother later. Take your time to check underneath the bar too.

13 The back of the brake levers should be double checked too, as this is your last chance to get this right before starting the finishing touches. The back of the lever should be properly covered. If there are gaps, undo the section and redo it, but be careful to unwrap the tape slowly, as you can rip it easily in frustration!

14 The final run of tape goes almost all the way to the centre of the bar. Where the centre section starts, there is usually a rise in the diameter. Unravel the last wrap and cut a straight edge from half-width to the front side of the bar. Cut a wedge shape away so it matches the angle of the wrapping.

15 For a smooth centre section, wrap the final turn around and behind the brake cable where it will tuck in smoothly. Once the end is finished off straight, wrap this up with a single thickness of insulating tape.

16 Leaving three-quarters of the width of the tape to overlap the hole at the start allows you to finish the bar end plugs neatly. Stuff the excess into the bar end by folding the ends of the tape into the open end of the bar. Crease the tape like this so that it maintains its position before inserting the end plug.

18 Lastly the rubber lever hoods will cover up the mess under the lever, but overlong covering pieces underneath will make the hood lumpy, so trim them down to the bare minimum and tape them into place with some electrical tape. Keep the bulk under the hoods tucked away or removed.

17 Then force the end plugs into the bar ends. They should push fit fairly easily – if they are very tight, trim a little of the excess off and try again.

FITTING PEDALS

Toe clips and straps are, thankfully, now a thing of the past. They were dangerous if tightened up too much. Most road cyclists now use clipless pedals, and there are countless different types and makes. The most popular are Look, Time, Speedplay and Shimano.

Historically, the first successful clipless pedal system arrived on the scene in 1985. Look were a ski company who realised that, to make a successful pedal system, the pedal has to rely on a cleat that snaps into a spring-loaded fastening, as a ski relies on the boot and the binding. Clipless pedals offer the most efficient power transfer – the cleat is screwed to the sole of the shoe, so they let you pull as well as push because you're clipped into the pedal.

1 Before you start, remember that pedals have a left- and right-handed thread. Most systems stamp 'L' and 'R' on the axle somewhere so you know which is which. On Shimano pedals, this is stamped on the flat part of the pedal spindle, where the spanner attaches.

2 Pedal threads must be greased. Use a good-quality, water-proof synthetic or anti-seize grease. Clean the threads and re-grease them regularly. Because axles are made out of steel and cranks are made out of aluminium, there can be problems with threads seizing. Also, be careful not to cross-thread the cranks, as they can easily be ruined.

3 Left- and right-hand pedal threads tighten up in the direction of pedalling. The easiest way to remember this is to hold the pedal up to the crank, flat on your fingers, and spin the cranks backwards as if you were freewheeling.

4 Some pedals have Allen-key fittings, and these usually require a long Allen key to either tighten correctly or, more importantly, provide enough leverage to remove.

5 Tighten the pedals to the manufacturer's recommended torque setting. Hold the opposite crank or the rear wheel and use the added leverage to help you tighten the pedals.

6 To remove the pedals, it's probably easiest if you stand the bike on the floor. You'll remove the pedal in the direction of the freewheel, so you may have to hold the opposite crank to prevent it from spinning.

7 If you're using clipless pedals for the first time (and they have tension adjustment), back the springs right off, so that the release tension is minimal. This helps getting used to the system and enables you to get out easily to put your foot down. Over the first few days you can tighten them.

8 As Speedplay pedals are double-sided, they're a lot easier for first-time users – there's no need to 'flip the pedals' to step into them. The cleats are the spring-and-release system.

PEDAL CLEATS

Once you've installed the pedals, you can fit the cleats to your shoes. Most shoes adopt the three-bolted system, which makes it easiest to set the angle of cleat and retain a solid fixing for the step-out flick. Make sure that the bolts are the right length and don't protrude into the sole.

Look to align your feet in the way you walk. Foot alignment is becoming a very serious business and most good bike-fitters will now recommend that you see a podiatrist to get custom-made footbeds, which provide stability and align your feet for more efficient pedalling. The pedal axle needs to be directly under the ball of your foot, so spend time and get it right. Regular cleaning and lubrication are essential. Always pick out any of the jammed-in mud and grit from around the cleat, as it can prevent stepping out of the binding.

Walking in road-shoe plates wears the cleats out quickly and is pretty dangerous anyway. Rubber covers are available for most pedal systems, and they'll prevent slipping on hard floors and avoid wear to the cleat. Worn cleats are likely to release easily and when you least expect them to (in a sprint!).

1 Assess the position of the ball of your foot over the pedal axle. Mark on the side of your shoe where the ball of your foot is, then mark a line across the sole of your shoe. This is where the cleat will be placed. Use this reference to decide which set of holes in the plates to use.

2 Prepare the threads in the plates with copper slip. The cleats will rust pretty quickly if you don't. You can replace these screws with stainless steel bolts (you can buy these from an engineering supplier), as they're less likely to rust up and will therefore last longer.

3 Most systems have slotted washers to allow plenty of fore and aft adjustments. A light grease on these will help keep them easy to adjust.

4 Tighten the shoe cleats to the recommended torque setting. Don't over-tighten them, as the threads can strip very easily, in which case you would have to replace the sole insert. Check the bolts regularly, as they can shake loose.

5 The correct cleat position is with the ball or pushing part of your foot over the pedal axle. This requires measuring and some trial and error to get spot-on. It's also best to get someone to help you do this job, as you can only adjust the cleat position properly once the cleats are in place.

6 Speedplay cleats have a four-bolt fitting cleat and they're supplied with a plate that fixes to the three-bolt-pattern shoe. The cleats are also the sprung part of the system and need regular cleaning and lubricating (use a very lightweight oil). The cleat bolts should be Loctited into place, as they cannot be too tight. Over-tightening the bolts will prevent the springs from moving and therefore prevent the float.

7 Time pedals now have the same three-bolt pattern cleat fitting as Look and other manufacturers. The brass cleat snaps into the pedal-binding and needs to be kept clean.

PEDAL TIPS

1   Noisy or creaking pedals can be due to worn cleats or simply dry threads. Re-grease the threads regularly and replace your cleats before they start to release on their own. It's not only annoying, it can also be dangerous.

2   If your cleats are shaking loose regularly, use some Loctite on the pedal-bolt threads, especially if you ride on cobbles!

3   The cleat will wear more quickly on the side you release most often when you stop, so swap cleats around periodically (if they're not left- and right-specific).

4   Pedal washers may be supplied with some cranks, especially carbon cranks. These are intended for use with pedals that don't have a round shoulder (usually cheap pedals) where the flats are exposed. These can otherwise bite into the crank and damage the carbon.

5   Regular cleaning and lubrication are essential. Dirty pedals become sticky to get out of and can seize completely. Never walk across mud or grass, as the muck can bung up the sensitive spring system.

6   Binding as you pedal and loose bearings are usually the telltale signs of a bent axle. Replace axles after a crash – extensive spares are usually available.

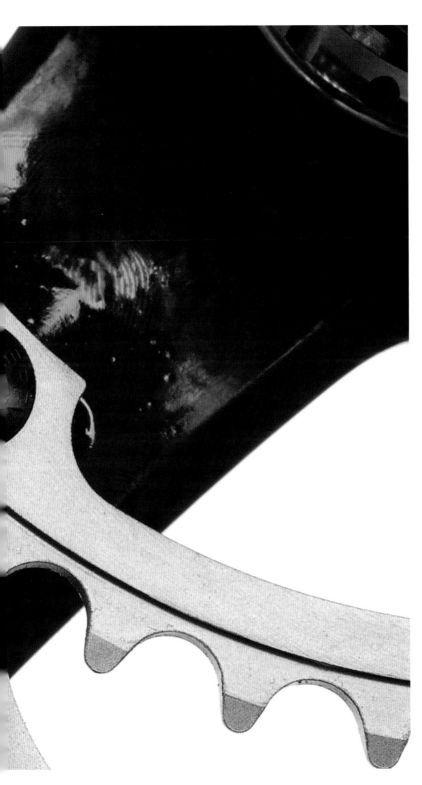

09

DRIVETRAIN

Chainrings and cranks combine to form the chainset, and these are the engine room of the bike – that is, the bit that gets all the power directly from your legs and helps you rip up the road. There are now several systems available, and most manufacturers have a solution for the chainset and bottom bracket (BB) unit.

Compatibility is always the main issue. For example, Campagnolo square-taper won't work with Shimano square-taper BB axles and vice versa. ISIS drive was developed by a group of smaller manufacturers who kept to the same design for inter-compatibility. External bearing cups are now the future, and most big manufacturers are making a system like this.

(See also pages 94-95 for more on External BBs.)

CHAINSETS, CRANKS AND CHAINRINGS

You'll always have to buy from the same manufacturer for crank and BB, although some small specialist engineering companies (like Royce) make custom BBs to fit practically all makes of crank to date. Most manufacturers use an integrated system that means the chainset is held in a preset position on the axle. This ensures perfect alignment of the drivetrain.

'Adjustable' brackets with lock-rings are better for cranks that may require moving from side to side to attain the best position or chainline – they can then be set into position using a lock-ring on either side.

Q FACTOR

This is the distance across the pedal faces, i.e. how wide apart your legs are. This should be approximately 145mm (5.7in) for road bikes. You can't go much narrower or the cranks hit the chainstays. A wide Q factor is bad because all your joints have to compensate – your knees get especially abused and bend the wrong way with a wider Q factor.

TOOLS REQUIRED

1. Allen keys
2. Crank-puller and spanner
3. Torque wrench and 8mm Allen socket
4. Copper slip
5. Chainline tool
6. Lock-ring tools
7. Vice or large spanner

A short BB axle is stiffer and lighter. You also get good ankle-clearance with a short BB and a low-profile crank. A 122mm BB is always going to give you a bigger Q factor and therefore a more flexible power transfer.

CRANK ARMS

The crank arm has to be really stiff – this is an absolute priority. Stamping and pulling on a strong crank relays all the power you can muster to the rear wheel, while flexible cranks are inefficient and are more likely to break unexpectedly. Their shape should be smooth and flowing, and there should be no sudden changes in shape or section. Sharp pockets and cut-out areas cause stress risers and cracks to start, leading to eventual breaks.

CRANK LENGTH

Usually, road crank arms are either 170mm, 172.5mm or 175mm long. The one you use is up to you – there are no set rules – but it'll also be governed very slightly by your leg-length. 175mm cranks give better leverage but aren't ideal for riders shorter than 1.7m (5ft 7in) tall. Most manufacturers will put 170mm crank arms on smaller bikes for this reason. Track cranks can be 165mm for clearance and also for 'spinning up' the gear. Smaller riders and female riders may also prefer shorter cranks.

SPIDER

Part of the same five-arm forging that holds the chainrings to the crank, spiders are on the drive side. Flexible spiders allow the chainrings to move when the front mech tries to shift, giving you sloppy shifts, and bent or out-of-line spiders will make the gears rough and upset the shifting.

The spider is probably the most important area of the drivetrain for two reasons – first, it's responsible for the accurate alignment of the rings to the rear cassette (chainline), and secondly, it needs to be super-stiff and totally flex free for power transfer to the rear wheel.

REMOVING STANDARD SQUARE-TAPER CRANKS

Removing cranks is simple, as long as you use the right tools. Replacing cartridge BBs couldn't be easier, so if you're still running a cup and loose ball-bearing bracket, you should think about changing soon. A lot of BBs are 'fit-and-forget' units, i.e. once it's in, you don't need to worry about it. (See pages 94-5 for more on BBs.)

1 On standard cranks, the fixing bolt has an 8mm Allen head with the washer as an integral part of the bolt. Old-style cranks still use a 14mm or 15mm hex-headed bolt and washer that can be protected by a separate dust cap.

2 The bolt has a washer/cover around it to protect the threads inside the crank. There may also be a washer (usually on Campagnolo only) behind the bolt, so make sure that you remove this also.

3 Once you've removed the bolts and washers, remove the crank using a crank-puller. This tool is essential for taking the cranks off the bike, and good ones won't damage the threads or the end of the axle. Clean out any dirt from the crank threads with a squirt of spray-lube.

4 The crank-puller has a central bolt, and once it's threaded into the crank as far as it'll go, the central bolt can be tightened to 'push' the crank away from the BB axle. Undo the centre bolt first so it fits as flush as possible, being careful to get it in straight.

5 The easiest puller to use is one with an arm attached to the end of the centre bolt – they are useful for travelling toolkits when you might not have room for a big spanner. However, it's worth noting that most pullers accept a 15mm spanner, so you can use a pedal-spanner to tighten the removing bolt.

TIP

Carefully tighten the crank-puller, ensuring it's inserted well into the crank thread – tightening the puller by just a few threads or cross-threading it can strip out the threads when you tighten the centre bolt to pull off the crank, rendering your crank useless.

6 ISIS and Octalink cranks have a hollow round axle and therefore require a larger head on the crank-puller – Park's remover can accept either types and is supplied with a pair of different-sized adaptors. ISIS axles have a symmetrical splined pattern on the axle, and it's worth cleaning this every time you remove the crank arms. Shimano Octalink cranks are very different, so don't try to mix them up.

7 Once you've correctly inserted the puller, tighten the arm (or central bolt) towards the BB axle. The arm rests on the end of the axle and the pushing/pulling motion forces the crank off the square-axle taper. The crank will try to drop off onto the floor, so be careful to keep hold of it.

8 Some cranks have 'captive' bolts. These have a puller built in, and the crank bolt is held captive so that the undoing action of the crank bolt also removes the crank for you. These are recommended on ISIS and Octalink, and are also fitted to some Shimano cranksets.

9 Removing captive-bolted cranks just requires one 8mm Allen key. They're a great idea for touring bikes and commuters, solving extra tool-carrying problems.

10 Always retighten cranks to the recommended torque setting and check them after the first ride, as they can loosen off slightly due to the pedalling force.

MAIN BB/CHAINSET TYPES

- JIS Square Taper (Japanese Industry Standard) – Shimano and Far-Eastern manufacturers standard square taper BB fitting.

- Campagnolo Square Taper – as used by Campagnolo up until 2007.

- Octalink – Shimano's step away from the square taper; used a bigger BB axle and a machined keyway fitting.

- ISIS Drive – the International Splined Interface Standard (all manufacturers except Campagnolo and Shimano).

- External Bearing – Shimano's Hollowtech II and Truvativ (SRAM).

- Ultra-Torque – Campagnolo's take on the external bearing BB and crank system. (See page 178 for more on Ultra-Torque.)

CHAINRINGS

Fitting chainrings is very simple, but make sure that you get the correct size for your crank. Chainrings come in hundreds of sizes and are made in a variety of manufacturing processes – stamped, CNC-machined and sometimes part-cut/part-machined. The current trend is for ramps and rivets to assist the chain in shifting. The usual drive set-up will be 53-/39-toothed rings, but any number of combinations are possible on most cranks.

RING SIZES

PCD (or BCD) stands for Pitch Circle Diameter (or Bolt Circle Diameter). This dimension varies according to manufacturer. Campagnolo uses a 135mm PCD, which means the smallest ring they can manage is a 39-tooth. Shimano uses a smaller, 130mm PCD, but this still only allows a smallest inner ring of 38 teeth. There are many other sizes depending on manufacturer – some older cranks (and various track cranks) can be 144mm, so bear this in mind when buying new chainrings. The latest compact road cranks have a 110mm PCD, which means they can get down to a 34-tooth inner chainwheel. (See more on chainring sizes in 'Compact Cranks' on page 174.)

CHAINRING BOLTS

Chainring bolts are made from steel, titanium or aluminium. Steel bolts are probably the best, as they're cheap and strong. They need greasing every now and then, as they can seize if left to rust. Use copper grease on the bolts. Titanium bolts are very light but very expensive, and also require special attention if left for long periods of time, as they can seize up. Aluminium bolts are really light but not very strong, and can snap off. Use plenty of copper slip or anti-seize compound on them and only tighten to the manufacturer's recommended torque setting.

Chainring bolts should be tightened gradually and in sequence (that is, not from left to right but from opposite bolt to opposite bolt). This is so that you don't over-tighten them and to ensure that the rings run true. There's one set for the two large chainwheels and one set for the granny ring (if you have a triple).

FITTING CHAINRINGS

1 All chainrings will have an alignment arrow, which usually lines the chainrings up with the crank. Another giveaway to orientation on the outer (big) chainwheel is a chain pip – an aluminium grommet that stops the chain getting jammed between the spider and the crank, should the chain unship.

2 The inner chainwheel may also have an orientation mark (especially if it's on a triple crank, and the ring has grooves and ramps for the chain to shift along). Usually, the graphics on the outside of both chainrings will have been designed to line up. Once the rings are aligned correctly, hold them together with the first bolt as they're unlikely to be able to stay in place.

3 On Campagnolo Record cranks, one of the bolts threads directly into the crank arm. There's a spacer and a shim to provide exact alignment, so be careful to reinstall these when reassembling them, and place this bolt in first.

4 Use a decent-quality grease or copper slip on the bolts and directly into the bolt-holes. Not only does this prevent the bolts from seizing, but also stops them 'drying out' and creaking as time goes by.

5 Most chainring bolts take a 5mm Allen key and need to be tightened to 6Nm (aluminium) or 10Nm (steel).

6 Torq key fittings are now being used on new Campagnolo cranks, so be sure to use the right tools and carry them with you in your toolkit.

7 Chainring bolts can rotate in the crank, so use a bolt-wrench to hold the nut at the back and prevent it from spinning.

COMPACT DRIVE CRANKS

Compact drive is a very sensible option for anyone who likes riding a road bike for training and pleasure, but doesn't necessarily want to race. Indeed, many new bikes are now coming with a compact drive set-up as standard, and this is a welcome trend for riders who are more interested in riding 'comfortably' than they are about racing. It's all about having enough gears for the hills, so compact can help without adding extra weight.

It allows you to retain the clean road bike lines and keeps the bike looking less cluttered than with a triple set-up. All the installation and servicing of compact cranks is the same, but there are a few things that you need to know. What about racing on compact? Yes, this is possible – even pro riders have been known to use compact ratios for very steep mountain stages in the Giro d'Italia (Tour of Italy) and Vuelta a España (Tour of Spain). The gear ratios can allow riders to spin a more comfortable cadence and stay seated longer. Compact chainrings are usually sized 50/34 or 50/36.

A triple drivetrain can weigh more than a double set-up. Campagnolo and Shimano now offer triple groupsets at Record, Chorus and Dura-Ace, and Ultegra, but you have to ask yourself whether it's really necessary. Also, some frames struggle to accept a triple crank, as they've been designed specifically to be used with a

double. Fitting a longer BB axle is possible, but it can just mess up the chainline, making gear-shifting poor and placing further strain on the drivetrain. So, you may be better off with Compact, especially on a racing frame with close clearances.

RING SIZES

The latest Compact road cranks

have a 110mm PCD which means they can get down to a 34-tooth inner chainwheel.

WEIGHT COMPARISON

Generally speaking, a triple group weighs about 200g more than a standard double. There are too many variables, so a standard benchmark isn't really possible – but for example, the

GEAR RATIO RANGE COMPARISON (USING 12–25 TOOTH CASSETTE)

Gear length is measured by the distance a bike travels with one pedal revolution.

Double compact with 50/34 rings	35.7in–109.5in	(90.7cm–278.1cm)
Double 'Standard' with 53/39 rings	42.1in–119.3in	(106.9cm–303.0cm)
Triple with 52/42/30 rings	31.5in–113.9in	(80.0cm–289.3cm)

It's worth noting that a double chainring set-up also allows more 'usable' gears than on a triple, i.e. gears which the chainline can handle more efficiently, while providing less doubling-up of ratios. You get fewer actual gears in total, but 20 is enough, isn't it?

new Campagnolo Record Ultra-Torque Compact set-up (with double crank) is under 750g, while a good-quality triple crank and BB will weigh around 1kg. This represents a 250g saving, which is about the weight of a front hub.

GEARING

Be honest, how often do you use 53×12 anyway? A 50×11 is still a massive gear in anyone's book – combine it with a 36-tooth inner chainring and a 11–25 cassette, and you'll be able to bomb up hills as well as down them. In fact,

if you fit 50×11, you'll achieve a gear of 119in (302cm), which is a bigger gear than 53×12 at 116in (295cm). (See page 112 for more on cassettes and gear ratios.)

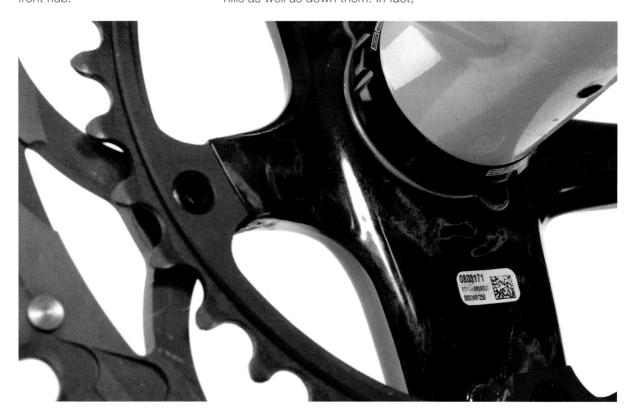

FRONT MECH

Dropped chains can be a problem when using a Compact drive system. A standard road front mech is designed with a larger plate-size, to be used with a 52/42 combination or the more popular 53/39. Campagnolo have a special front mech called the CT, and this is designed with a smaller inner plate so it shifts better and holds the chain on.

However, the usual reason for a dropped chain is a poor chainline and badly matching components. Stick with one brand and keep things simple, without too many big jumps in gear sizes.

Fitting a chain-retainer is a good idea. Usually called 'chain-watchers', they're plastic clips that sit inside the inner chainwheel where a hook prevents the chain from dropping. These devices are often used by pro mechanics when setting up odd gear ratios.

REAR MECH CAPACITY

This will depend on the ratios you're running on your cassette and chainrings. Most shifting problems start when the chain is placed under shifting pressure and the mech cannot cope with the pressure. Work the capacity out as follows:

11–25 cassette
(subtract 11 from 25) = 14T

50/36 chainrings
(subtract 36 from 50) = 14T

Then add the two together – in this case, the total capacity required is 28 teeth.

The bigger the ratios, the longer the arm (or cage) of the rear mech you'll require – this allows for the slack in the longer chain to be accounted for by the arm. This is why triple set-ups need a long-arm mech to work properly with wide-ratio gears.

Shimano short-cage road mechs usually have a capacity of 29 teeth, which means you could run a 50/36 chainring and a 12–27 cassette. Campagnolo short-cage rear mechs can cope with 28 teeth, so they work best with a 50/36 crank and a 12–25 cassette. This will also cope with closer ratios, so if you wanted a racing ratio you could just swap the cassette for an 11–23, for example. I'd suggest that if you prefer Campagnolo and want to swap between cassette ratios, go for the mid-length mech as it can cope with 30 teeth (Campagnolo do three types, and the longest has a capacity of 39 teeth).

BB

This is where most mistakes are made. Don't compromise by trying to use any bracket that happens to be fitted to your bike. Get the bracket that the crank manufacturer recommends (easy to find on their websites) and ask a shop mechanic to help if you're in doubt. Current designs of BBs have made it easier to have two cranks and change (Shimano Hollowtech and Campagnolo Ultra-Torque). Sliding cranks in and out is easy, with only small adjustments needed to the front mech.

There are several opinions on wear and tear with Compact drivetrains. Many riders say that Compact drive wears chains and sprockets faster than a triple.

This is partly due to using the wrong combination of components and a front mech that cannot cope with the front shift. It can also be due to running the chain too short or using inappropriate gear combinations (e.g. big ring to big sprocket). However, a completely compatible drivetrain (chainrings, chain, cassette and mechs) will prevent much of the hassle.

FITTING CRANKS

CAMPAGNOLO ULTRA-TORQUE

Ultra-Torque cranks rely on an axle which joins in the centre of the BB axle. Like Shimano's, this is a very simple yet strong solution to fastening the cranks into the frame. The bearings are sealed and outboard of the frame, and they allow for an oversized-diameter axle for greater stiffness and efficiency.

The whole unit is held in place with a 10mm Allen-key bolt located in the centre of the BB axle joining the two halves of the axle, which has a set of locking teeth to maintain a close join. This means that there's only one fixing for the whole system and ensures simplified fitting and ease of service.

As with Shimano, the frame's BB shell needs to be tapped and faced, so as to offer exact fitting for the BB cups. The Ultra-Torque system is designed to fit Italian-threaded BB shells with a width range of 69.2–70.8mm, and English-threaded BB shells with a width range of 67.2–68.8mm. If your frame is outside of these dimensions, you may have to face down the bracket (if it's too wide) or fit spacers (if it's too narrow).

1 First, the BB cups install into the frame in the same way as Shimano's and using the same pattern spanner. Tighten to the cups to 35Nm.

2 Grease the insides of the cups where the bearing units will sit. Use a lightweight grease, just to prevent the bearings from seizing or water sitting inside the cups.

3 The drive-side crank is inserted first. The bearing is factory fitted to the inside of the cranks and can be replaced.

4 Push the crank into the BB cups so that the bearing fits flush with the edge of the cups.

5 Once the drive-side bearing is in place, you can fit the spring clip – this prevents the drive side from falling out when you insert the left-hand crank. Wiggle the cranks to make sure that the spring clip has retained the bearing properly.

6 Line up the left-hand crank with the drive-side crank – it's possible to fit the cranks 'wonky', as the serrated mating point is symmetrical. There's also a washer (already inside the BB cup in this picture) that needs to fit over the BB axle.

7 As with the drive side, the left-hand crank-side bearing fits flush with the BB cup and is sealed with a rubber seal.

8 Once lined up, it should be very easy to push the two crank sides together – the axle will mesh perfectly inside the BB shell.

9 Apply some grease to the thread of the bolt and, with a socket-set extension bar, pass the bolt into the hole on the drive side of the assembly, then locate the thread in the centre of the axle.

10 Tighten the bolt with a torque wrench. The correct tightening torque is 42Nm. To remove the cranks, simply undo this bolt and pull the left-hand crank away. Then remove the spring clip and remove the drive side.

SRAM/TRUVATIV CRANKS

1 SRAM cranks use a similar system to Shimano's, but like Campagnolo, it's a one-bolt fitting unit. The cups fit in the same way and use the same pattern-spanner as Shimano and Campagnolo.

2 The axle is attached to the drive side and passes through the two cups. Apply a little grease to the parts that come into contact with the bearings.

3 Simply slide the axle through the cups and push the crank against the bearing on the drive side.

4 There's an ISIS-style fitting on one end of the axle and this will protrude from the cups to allow the left-hand crank to tighten onto, and secure, the system in one action.

5 There's an aluminium sleeve on the inside of the left-hand crank, inside the carbon arm, which requires a little grease on the inside to prevent it from seizing.

6 There's a simple captive bolt on the left-hand crank, which tightens the whole system and also removes the crank in one, so as you undo the bolt the cranks will pull off the end of the axle.

BOTTOM BRACKET SERVICING AND FITTING

BBs come in a variety of lengths, sizes and specifications. They're either standard square-taper, ISIS, Octalink or 'through-axle' fittings like Campagnolo Ultra-Torque or Shimano Hollowtech II. (If you have a through-axle, turn to page 178 for specific information on these types.)

Earlier versions, which used loose ball-bearing cup-and-axle, required attention even after the smallest rainfall. They also needed the patience of a watchmaker to set up without play or dragging. However, in recent years the one-piece unit with sealed bearings and a fiddle-free cartridge housing has been developed and can be set up to be smooth-running and trouble-free.

All types of English-threaded BB unit thread into the BB shell of the frame, with the right-hand cup threading in anti-clockwise (as it's a left-hand thread) and the left-hand cup threading in clockwise (as it's a standard, right-hand thread).

ENGLISH OR ITALIAN?

The BB threads in most road bikes are 'English' pattern (marked '1.370in × 24 TPI'). Some bikes (mainly Italian-brand road bikes) have 'Italian' threads (marked '36 × 24in'), which are slightly larger in diameter than the usual English bracket threads. Italian threads are also both right-hand threads on the drive and non-drive side. Always check the size on the side of the bracket cups before you start to adjust.

Most standard Shimano units are sealed disposable units, which need completely replacing when they wear out. However, with a few more expensive brackets you can replace the bearings, in a similar way to cartridge-bearing hubs. (See pages 70-72 for more on cartridge bearing hubs.)

SQUARE–TAPER BBS

On a square-taper BB, a two-degree angled taper is machined on four faces of the axle to give you a tight, precision fit into the square-tapered holes in the alloy cranks. This is a fairly standard engineering technique and gives a large contact area at the connection between the cranks and the axle. Check that the fit is correct for your crank

when buying a new BB. The usual cause of creaking cranks is either dirt in this area, or an incompatible fit.

Octalink and ISIS systems use a splined axle that is oversized and therefore less vulnerable to twisting forces than the standard square taper. They're also slightly lighter. However, they've now been superseded by the larger-diameter (and even lighter) through-axle cranks. However, many smaller brands still use ISIS and Octalink fittings and BBs.

The central sleeve of a sealed BB keeps the bearings sealed from the water and dirt that can get into the inside of the BB via the frame tubes. The sleeve also acts as an accurate spacer to hold the cups and bearings in the correct position – they're usually made from aluminium or plastic. Lock-rings are not always necessary in modern cassette-type brackets, as they have a standard-width fit.

BOLTS AND THREADS

The BB axle has threads tapped into either end of it for accepting the crank bolts. The crank bolts are normally Allen-key bolts set in plastic washers (to seal the crank extractor threads), or the captive bolt system, which enables the crank to be removed in the loosening action. Older cranks may have a 14mm or 15mm bolt, which requires a socket spanner to remove.

AXLE LENGTH

The axle length will depend on the type of crank you're using. Standard BB axles come in a

TOP: SHIMANO OCTALINK. ABOVE: STANDARD CAMPAGNOLO SQUARE TAPER

huge range of lengths, from 103mm to 124mm. When you replace a unit, always use the same-length axle. Shorter axles can mean that the chainrings rub on the frame, while longer ones will mess up your chainline and your gears won't work. If you're fitting a new crank and BB, check with the manufacturer which axle length you'll need to match your old set-up.

If you ruin or cross-thread the threads in your BB, you can have it re-reamed and re-threaded to a larger size. A framebuilder can sometimes repair the threads too, but these jobs are best done by a qualified mechanic, as ruining the BB will usually mean your frame will be severely compromised and it'll be hard to service in the future.

Regardless of what type of drivetrain your bike has, failing to prepare the frame will mean that the BB unit won't sit properly in the bike. It may spin around okay, but once the cranks and chain are installed, a poorly prepared and fitted BB will damage the bearings, and the unit won't run efficiently.

FITTING STANDARD BOTTOM BRACKETS

1 Thread and BB preparation is essential. The tools needed to do this job are very expensive and require careful handling. This may mean you have to get a good bike shop to do the first few (cutting) tasks for you, but it's essential that the threads are cleaned and the faces squared up before you start.

2 The threads need to be thoroughly cleaned (use an old toothbrush and a strong degreaser). Remove any oxide build-up and then dry off completely. Dress the threads with a good-quality grease – waterproof greases are best – and use copper slip on titanium components. Some mechanics will use thread-lock on Italian BBs to prevent the cups from loosening, but be careful as this can create long-term problems.

3 The new unit will have one removable side, which is usually on the non-drive side. Pull this off, so that the unit can be installed into the drive side first. This side has a left-hand thread and tightens anti-clockwise.

4 The non-drive-side cup is right-hand threaded and is designed to be flange-less, so it can accommodate a variety of widths of BB. This tightens clockwise and will mesh with the cartridge inside the shell. Most Shimano brackets have a taper on the inside that allows it to self-locate. Again, tighten this with your fingers until there's about 1cm (1/2in) of thread left showing. If the threads have been properly prepared, you'll be able to turn the unit into place with your fingers. Spin it in until there's about 1cm (1/2in) of thread left on either side.

5 Shimano brackets use a special tool that sits in serrations around the edge of the cup. Some brackets use a set of holes that accept a pin spanner or peg tool and a lock-ring to hold it in position. If you don't get the right tools for the bracket, you risk making a mess of the unit and your frame.

6 Campagnolo BBs have a smaller ring of serrations and use the same remover as their cassettes. Be careful with poorly fitting or worn tools, as these can easily be rounded out if you don't take care.

7 The best tool to remove Campagnolo BBs is one that can be threaded into the ends of the BB axle and held 'captive'. These are much safer and easier when exerting plenty of pressure to remove stubborn units. Holding everything firmly in position like this leaves you free to get on with the job.

8 Next, use the BB tool to tighten the unit into the frame. Make sure that the shoulder of the unit on the drive side is tight up against the frame first. This is to make sure that the chainset will sit in the right place to achieve the most efficient chainline. With the flange flush to the frame, it won't loosen off.

9 Once the drive side is tight, you can tighten the non-drive side and lastly tighten both side cups to 40–50Nm (check manufacturer's recommendation). Clean up any excess grease around the frame and threads, then you can re-install the cranks. Replace the cable guide (the bolt may need shortening if you've fitted a different type of bracket). Don't tighten this bolt into the outside of the unit as it can damage the seal.

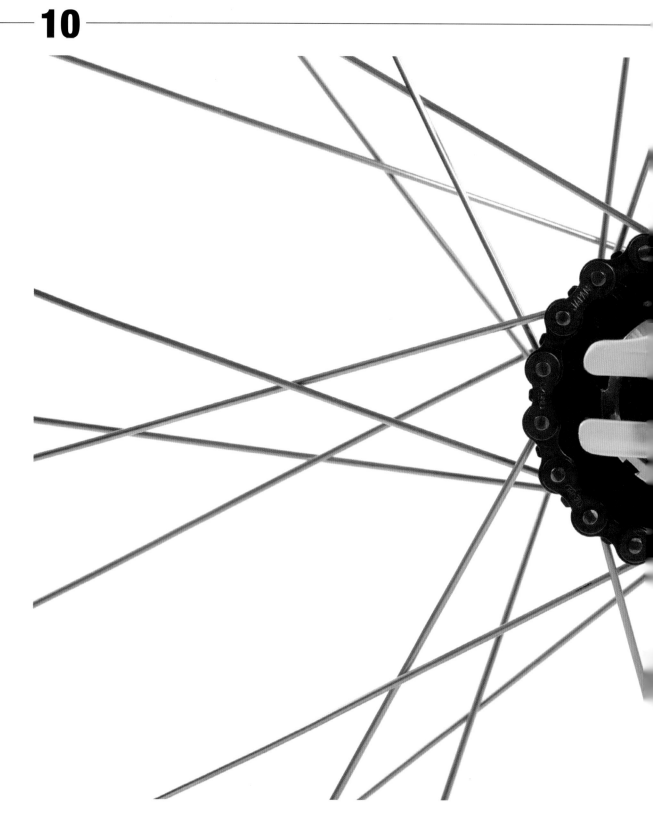

10

OTHER BIKES

One of the great aspects of road cycling is the diversity of the niches within the sport. From track riding to cyclo-cross there is a different bike for almost all eventualities. Where once riders made do with one bike, two at a push, now there's a load of excuses to get out to the bike shop and order another steed. Although the principles of the bikes remain the same there are some differences that set a cyclo-cross bike apart from a track pursuit bike.

TRACK BIKES – FIXED WHEEL

For racing, track bikes usually have an 89in or 90in (226cm or 229cm) gear – this is the distance that the bike travels with one pedal revolution. In simple terms, this is usually a 49-tooth chainring and a 14-tooth sprocket, or 50×15. This depends on many different conditions, and experienced track riders will 'gear up' or 'gear down' depending on the track, level of fitness and type of race that they're riding. It seems confusing at first, but gear ratios are all-important when racing the track. Many top riders have a bag of tools, sprockets and chainwheels that they take to the track centre so that they can change gear ratios quickly when the event demands it.

1 Fixed-wheel bikes use front and rear hubs with nuts rather than a QR skewer. Threaded nuts will hold the chain tension far longer than a QR skewer, which can slip. QR skewers are also not allowed on track race bikes.

2 Track bikes have rear-facing dropouts and 120mm-spaced hubs (rather than 130mm of a road bike). Rear-facing dropouts offer a stronger and simpler solution to adjusting chain tension and accommodating variations in sprocket (gear) sizes.

3 On fixed, always use a 1⁄8in chain (they're wider than a 3⁄32in mech one), and if you use a single chainring, check the chain tension regularly. Beefier track chains stay put if the chain wobbles a bit over bumps or when pedalling fast. 1⁄8in chains are practically indestructible.

4 This chain fastens with a screw and a nut on the other side – it isn't a problem that they stick out, as the chain doesn't pass through mechs. This makes it easier to remove and change chains, and it's handy for cleaning too.

5 Chainline and tension are all-important. A track single chain-wheel, mounted to a specific crank (Miche, TA, Shimano, Campagnolo, etc) and suitably matched BB is the best option to get the chainline accurate. To get the chainline spot-on, it's best to get a specific track crank and matching BB, like this Campagnolo set-up.

6 You must line up the chain so that the sprocket is directly behind the chainring, especially if you're riding fixed, as the chain may unship if the chainline is wrong. To adjust the chainline, you may have to change the BB axle or fit an adjustable BB that can be moved from side to side slightly.

7 To remove the wheel, slacken the wheel nuts fully and slide the wheel forwards in the dropouts. This will allow you to remove the chain from the chainring and the sprocket. Remove the chain from the sprocket and wrap around the seat stay as shown here – this will allow the wheel to be slid out backwards.

8 When returning the wheel to the bike, the chain can be wrapped over the chainring and sprocket. This will mean that the chain is too slack and you'll have to re-tension the drive. If the chain is sagging at the top and bottom, like this, it's way too loose to ride on.

9 To tension the chain, pull the track nuts back in the dropouts with the chain on the sprocket and chainwheel. Then tighten the nuts up finger tight.

10 You can then use the 15mm track nut wrench. Pull firmly backwards on the wheel (this is best done in a work-stand or with someone to help) and 'nip' the track nuts on both sides of the bike.

11 You may have to centralise the rear wheel and fully tighten the drive side first. Make sure that the wheel is central at the seat stays and chainstays just behind the bottom bracket before fully tightening the non-drive side. Hold the wheel firmly in position as you re-tighten the wheel nuts.

12 The correct chain tension will allow the wheel to rotate easily, and this means running with a little slack in the chain. Loosening the nuts slightly and slapping the chain with your nut wrench will slacken the chain a little if it's too tight.

HUB AND SPROCKET SERVICING/ REPLACEMENT

1 The fixed-wheel hub has two threads. The larger inside thread for the sprocket is a right-hand thread and tightens as you pedal, the smaller diameter lock-ring thread is left-hand threaded, and prevents the sprocket undoing as you decelerate by easing back on the pedals.

2 Also fit a decent quality sprocket – Campagnolo, Surly and Shimano are expensive, but sprockets need to be perfectly round. It's worth the investment, as cheap pressed cogs aren't always round and can have tight spots, which wears your chain out.

3 Use a chain whip with a long handle to remove the sprocket. This is a right-hand thread and as such is tightened further with the pedaling action. So, removing it can take a fair bit of effort.

4 When replacing the sprocket, grease the inside of the sprocket before you spin it onto the hub. Tighten with the chain whip before riding.

5 The lock-ring fits over the sprocket and is a left-hand thread so it tightens anti-clockwise. Fully tighten this up against the sprocket using a C-spanner with a tooth that fits the sprocket snugly.

6 Once you've ridden the bike for a few laps of the track, the sprocket will be tightened properly onto the hub. Double-check that the lock-ring is tight against the sprocket so that it stays retained. You can do this with the wheel still in the bike with this type of C-spanner.

MORE TRACK BIKE TIPS

CHAIN CLEANING

Keep your chain very clean. This will prevent you making a mess of your hands every time you swap sprockets. Use a chain wax rather than a heavy oil, and keep a rag handy to clean up.

CRANK LENGTH

Track cranks usually come in 165mm or 170mm lengths. Shorter cranks are a must on tight-banked tracks for pedal clearance. They're also better for quick acceleration and spinning low gears very fast.

TYRE OPTIONS

Use tubular or sprint rims for racing, although good-quality tyres and tubes are OK for training, especially on concrete or tarmac tracks. If you're taking track seriously, tubulars are much

better. They're quicker than tyres, run at very high pressures and also are less likely to slide off the wheel in the event of a puncture. It goes without saying that tubulars should be very well glued for track racing. (See page 86 for more on fitting tubulars.)

LOCK-RINGS

Some experienced track riders remove the lock-ring from the rear hub. This is to allow the sprocket to spin off, should the chain come off and get tangled, which can cause a nasty accident. But, as

long as the tension is sufficient and the chainline good, it's highly unlikely that this will happen. This is not recommended for road use, as you can easily unravel the sprocket on long descents!

STIFF AND STRONG IS BEST

If you're taking track racing seriously, you need to use products and contact points that are strong and solid, first and foremost.

Handlebars should be steel if you're a sprinter, and pedal

systems should be secure (which is why sprinters still use toe clips and straps). Seat posts should also be strong, as they can endure a fair amount of pressure as you wind up for a sprint.

WHEELS

Top track riders use carbon-disc wheels at the rear and strong four-spoke carbon front wheels. They want a wheel that won't flex and which offers top aerodynamic efficiency. Endurance riders will opt for lighter components, but with reliability still a priority.

WINTER FIXED OR SINGLESPEED

Try to ride singlespeed from October to January. There are several reasons for this:

- It means you don't have to clean your bike very often.

- You can re-learn how to spin a gear effectively.

- You have an excuse for being slower.

- You learn how to spin a gear properly for faster acceleration and sprinting.

The winter is bad for your bikes. Gears and brakes need regular cleaning, and if you're putting plenty of commuter miles in, then chains and cassettes wear out at an alarming rate. And how fast should you be riding in the winter anyway?

I'd even suggest that there are a few riders who would benefit from some pedalling lessons. And if your 'big ring' wears out every few months, you could be missing something in your training and cycle-craft.

Fixed can also add another dimension to riding in the wet or in slippery conditions, offering better balance and speed control than a freewheel bike – one of the reasons to ride one in the snow and ice.

WINTER TRAINER AND 'BIKE ABOUT TOWN'

Sadly, off-the-peg singlespeed bikes with mudguard eyes and braze-on fittings for racks and water bottles are rare. However, some custom builders do make them. 'Pure' track racing bikes tend to be a bit twitchy for road use and you can't get mudguards on them, and brakes may be impossible to fit (no clearance, and undrilled forks and brake-bridge) – but the main problem with pure track bikes on the road is that they aren't too comfortable for long journeys.

FIX UP AN OLD FRAME

If you have an old steel road frame, you could consider having it renovated and returned to the road as a singlespeeder. This can be expensive, but if the bike is in good condition and made from decent materials (i.e. Reynolds 531), it could easily be 'fixed'.

Several framebuilders will offer this service, but sometimes it's worth considering that you can buy a new frame and fork for the price of the repair – it can just be a labour of love. Also, if you're riding fixed on the road, check that the frame will allow for pedal overlap.

Chain tension is also important, and the reason why vertical dropouts don't work so well with singlespeed, as you can't move the wheel fore and aft. You can buy singulator tension devices that attach to the rear gear-hanger and take up the slack in the chain – they work very well, but look untidy.

If you have to use a standard front-facing dropout, I wouldn't

use fixed, as the twisting forces involved with constant acceleration and deceleration can crack the dropouts if they aren't up to it. However, they'll be fine for running a single-geared freewheel set-up.

Ideally, go for a frame with track-style (horizontal/rear-facing) dropouts and 120mm track-hub-spacing. You can buy a fixed-hub converter for 130mm-spaced Shimano road hubs (Surly make this – it's called a Fixxer), or if you want freewheel only, try a singlespeed converter which allows you to fit a single sprocket from an old Shimano or Campagnolo cassette, and spacers, onto an eight- or nine-speed freehub body for single-gear use.

STURMEY ARCHER'S FIXED THREE-SPEED HUB GEAR IS AN EXCELLENT VARIENT ON FIXED-WHEEL WINTER RIDING

PEDAL OVERLAP AND BB HEIGHT

To accommodate constant pedalling for road conditions when riding fixed, the frame should have a high BB, and clearance between the feet and the front wheel (pedal overlap).

They aren't essential features, but are worth considering for perfect fixed-gear performance and safety when riding around tight corners, or fitting a set of mudguards.

WHAT SIZE GEAR FOR THE ROAD?

Use a 42×16 if you live in a flat area, or 42×18 if it's hilly. Some people push bigger gears, but it really doesn't make that much difference on the flat – you can cruise at 32–35kmh (20–22mph) easily if riding in a group on 42×18. But your rpm rate goes a bit bananas after that. Ride a freewheel unless you have

experience of riding fixed – you should certainly try fixed, but I don't use it often (my usual Sunday ride is always too lumpy). Larger sprockets seem to hold the chain better and don't seem to wear out so fast. 44×18 or 46×19 are quite good combinations for flat-terrain fixed use.

REVOLUTIONS PER MINUTE...

200rpm is the most I've seen anyone do, which was on a 38×16 downhill – madness. You'll normally spin at 90–100rpm and you'll feel slightly under-geared at first. But stick with it, as it gets better in time. Eventually you'll iron out the flat spots in your pedalling and become silky smooth.

FREE

A single freewheel is not a soft option (although diehard fixers won't agree). It has all the

benefits of fixed, but the ability to freewheel down hills is a welcome one, and especially important if you train in a group in the hills, as they won't be waiting for you at the bottom. Freewheel-conversion is also fairly straightforward on most road bikes.

USING DOUBLE ROAD CRANKS

You can change the chainring bolts to shorter ones on a double chainset and ditch the outer ring. It's a bit of a bodge as this may mean that you have to run the inner chainwheel on the inside of the chainset still, but retaining a good chainline is essential.

FIXED/FREE HUBS

Some fixed hubs have two sets of threads, and this allows you to have a fixed and a freewheel on the same wheel. Then you have the option to swap the wheel around for riding the hills or in a group.

CYCLO-CROSS

The main differences between a 'cross bike and a standard road bike are as follows:

- Fatter off-road tyres or tubulars.
- Cantilever brakes for increased mud and tyre clearance.
- More wheel clearance built into the frame.
- A longer wheelbase and slacker, relaxed frame angles for stability.
- A higher bottom bracket for clearing hurdles and obstacles.
- SPD-type mountain bike pedals and shoes for running in the mud and up sharp hills.

WHEEL CHOICE

This varies between racing and training and also for courses. Deep-section wheels are popular with the professional riders, who tend to ride very fast across mud or sand, where the deep-section wheel is less likely to be swamped by the mud, and also sheds mud faster and more easily.

Most road wheels are fine for off-road racing and they're strong, but be aware that mud and constant washing will deteriorate the bearings and freewheel mechanisms, so save your best wheels for the most important races.

THE PITS

At 'cross races, it's permitted to have a spare bike and wheels available, should you need to swap bikes if it's muddy or change wheels after a flat.

A clean bike is a huge advantage in the mud, and most experienced 'cross mechanics will clean and prep a bike in a matter of minutes so as to be ready when their rider reappears on the next lap. Even if you don't have a willing helper, a spare set of wheels is a great idea just so you can go the distance even after a flat.

KEEP IT SIMPLE

There's a temptation to build a 'cross bike as light as possible, for carrying and run-ups. Carbon forks are usually a reliable choice, but I'd steer clear of cheaper carbon parts, especially seat posts (for more on carbon, see pages 18-20). Using lighter parts may also make the bike less controllable in quick technical descents, where a heavier,

sturdier bike will soak up the rough stuff better, so you're better off avoiding carbon altogether.

TYRE CHOICE

Tyre reliability can have a big influence on race results. Low tyre pressure offers plenty of grip and is essential when riding sandy courses.

However, safe use of low tyre pressure is only really possible with tubular tyres. A trade-off worth considering is using tubs for muddier, more demanding courses where they're less likely to puncture.

Tubs or tyres? For racing, tubs offer a greater level of control and have the advantage of puncturing less than standard tyres, but they aren't as user-friendly as tyres and you need to change them regularly.

GEARS, BRAKES AND CABLES

1 Gear ratios are now far easier to attain using a compact crank (see page 174). Many riders run a single chainring to prevent losing the chain, then keep the cassette ratios wider to allow plenty of usable gears. Inevitably, steep hills mean hopping off and running anyway, so smaller climbing gears are not always an advantage.

2 Brake cable routing is tricky for cantilever brakes. Several methods have been used, but hangers that fit into the spacers on the fork steerer offer the best solution for the front brake.

3 At the rear brake, a seat clamp can provide a good anchor for the outer cable, and keeps the rear triangle free of extra mud-clogging attachments.

4 Cross-top brake levers are very popular as the brakes can be operated when the rider is sitting upright and away from the brake levers.

5 Cross-top levers interrupt the cable-run, and the lever pulls on the outer cable to activate the inner, and therefore the brakes. They don't add much weight and do offer better control in technical sections.

6 Adding an adjuster for the gear cables at the shifter is a good idea. This will allow adjustment 'on the fly', as most cyclo-cross frames don't have a frame-mounted gear adjuster like road bikes do.

7 They can also be added into the cable-routing on the top tube – this barrel adjuster is very easy to fit and can easily be operated with winter gloves on.

8 Choose your brakes carefully. Standard MTB brakes are not ideal, as they're low-profile and designed for MTB levers. Cyclo-cross brakes are best when they have a lot of leverage and tyre clearance – braking power is not always the priority, especially in the mud. These Avid brakes have V-brake style pads that can be adjusted to allow for toe-in and to increase power.

9 Many off-the-shelf brakes have a standard set-distance straddle-wire – these work OK, but are not perfect for accurate adjustment and cable efficiency. They tend to sit very close to the tyres too, and attract a lot of dirt and debris.

10 Fit a standard yoke with a separate straddle-wire, as this will allow you to set the straddle further away from the tyres and adjust the feel of the brake. They also allow the brakes to be fully released when removing wheels quickly.

11 To remove the wheel, you have to unhook the straddle-wires, squeeze the pads together and unhook the straddle cable end.

12 Once the cable is unhooked, both sides of the brake fall away and will allow any tyre to be removed easily – this would be impossible with a standard calliper brake.

13 Most cantilever brakes are pretty basic, but brakes with added adjustments built in are increasingly available. These Avid brakes have a tension-adjuster to allow you to centre the brake and adjust the feel at the lever. Use an Allen key to adjust them and keep the pads perfectly aligned with the rims. Tightening the adjuster screw also increases the spring tension, which moves the pad away from the rim and increases the effort required to move the levers.

TIME TRIAL (TT) AND TRIATHLON

A time trial (TT) bike is much the same as a triathlon bike, although for Ironman races and longer hilly events a slightly more upright road-inspired position is preferred. Also the gearing may be more suited to the terrain.

And it's not as simple as getting the front end as low as you can manage. Chris Boardman's TT bike was set at such an extreme position that riders of a similar stature would struggle to ride for ten minutes on it, but as he points out, he's a peculiar shape and can sit happily

in an aero-tuck while riding to the shops. But not everyone is so lucky. Compare his position to Miguel Indurain, Fabian Cancellara or Tony Martin – these three superb TT riders can't achieve the same aero-tuck, but they go just as fast because they harness their power through a more efficient position.

Triathlon or Aero handlebars allow a rider to get into the appropriate aero time-trialling position. These handlebars first came about in the RAAM (Race Across America) and were actually intended for comfort at first, as they allowed the riders to rest their arms on the arm pads and still steer the bike.

But the result is not only comfortable, it's also very aerodynamic, allowing the rider to assume a downhill skiing-type tuck, with the arms providing a penetrating element for a much more aerodynamic shape.

Triathletes adopted the RAAM position to great effect, and it eventually reached mainstream cycling when Greg LeMond used these bars to win the Tour de France in dramatic style on the final-day TT in 1989, when he beat Laurent Fignon (who rode a standard bike) by just eight seconds overall – the closest-ever margin of victory.

BAR AND TRIATHLON-BAR SET-UP

1 Obviously, you have limits to how low you can go, and tri-bar rest-height and reach are often set at extremes – however, too long can affect the steering, and if you opt to place the gear controls at the bar-ends you may find that they're a bit of a stretch. Arm and torso length will play a part, as will your height and leg length.

2 Most stems will only allow a certain amount of adjustment, but if you're converting an old road frame to TT duties, the front end may be too high. Adjustable stems are a good idea to get the front end lower and gain aero advantage.

3 However, with too low a bar height, you may well experience neck and back pain the longer the event goes on for. It's worth considering a higher bar position (or even using a road bike set-up) if you're going to ride further than 80km (50mi). Use a set of bars that allow for a lot of adjustment at first so you can experiment and adapt your position.

OTHER COMPONENTS

Close gear ratios are less of a problem these days, as 10-speed cassettes will offer a wide spread of gears, albeit with jumps of just one or two sprockets. Pro bike riders will usually fit a larger chainring (54 or even 55 teeth) and a smaller inner chainring (48 or 50), thus keeping a very close set of ratios, but also keeping mainly high gears for quicker riding.

Specialist wheels are an obsession of all top time trial riders. Unless you're travelling at more than 40kmh (25mph), disc wheels and deep-section aero-wheels may be an expense you could do without. Tyres can make a bigger difference – opting for a comfortable yet quick set of tyres will certainly reduce rolling resistance and increase speed.

On pro TT bikes, brake levers are mounted in the end of the handlebar. These are usually aero-shaped and offer adequate braking (especially as you're trying to avoid braking to keep your speed up!).

With saddle height, the popular opinion has always been that a TT bike should have a higher saddle position than a road set-up, but recent research states exactly the opposite. The lower the position at the front, the further the saddle height needs to be. By leaning further over and, consequently, further forward of your usual road position, you're tilting your hips forwards more, which effectively lengthens the pedalling stroke and effectively raises your saddle height for you. A reduction of up to 2cm (1in) in saddle height is sometimes needed to retain the same power output when in the TT tuck.

GLOSSARY

Aheadset – bearing unit for forks, utilising an unthreaded steerer

axle vice – device for holding axles without damaging threads

ball-peen hammer – engineering hammer with a rounded end

barrel adjuster – threaded adjuster that can be turned with the fingers

BB axle – bottom bracket axle

bench-mounted grinder – electric grinder that mounts to a workbench

bottle cage bosses – threaded inserts into frame to allow bottle cage to be attached

bottom bracket shell – the part of the frame that houses the bottom bracket bearings

bottom bracket tapping and facing kit – the tools for preparing threads and faces of the bottom bracket shell

bottom bracket threads – threads inside the bottom bracket shell

bottom brackets – generic term for the bearing and axle for the chainset

brake bridge – part of the frame for hanging the brake from

brake calliper pivots – the points on the brake caliper that pivot

brake shoes – metal-retaining parts of the brake pads

braking surface – flat part of the rim that is used to brake

cable doughnuts – small rubber grommets that prevent cables from damaging the frame and paintwork

cadence – speed of pedaling (measured in rp/m)

callipers – the brake parts at the wheel

cantilever brakes – a type of brake used on cyclo-cross and touring bikes for increased tyre clearance

captive-bolted cranks – cranks with bolts that, when undone, will self-remove the crank

carbon steerers – the fork steerer made from carbon

cartridge brake shoes – where you can use replaceable brake blocks rather than the entire unit

cassette – usually referring to the rear gear sprockets (gear cogs) it is the cluster of cogs

cassette body – the part of the hub that the cassette attaches to

cassette carrier – the type of gear system used

cassette lock rings – for tightening and retaining the cassette to the rear hub

cassette sprockets – the individual gear cogs

chain checker – device used to check the wear of a chain

chain hanger – a frame part (or additional spare part) used to retain the chain (usually attached to the inside of the seat stay)

chain tool – or riveter used to remove and replace chain rivets when breaking or replacing a chain

chain whip – a small section of chain attached to a handle, for holding sprockets when undoing cassette lockrings

chainline – the angle of the chain between front chainring and rear sprocket

chainline gauge – tool used to set or check chainline

chainstays – the two frame tubes that connect the bottom bracket shell to the rear dropouts

chainwheel or chainring – the front cog of the drivetrain

chorus groupset – a type of Campagnolo product groupset

clipless pedals – pedal system that enables the shoes to be secured to the bike without clips and straps

compact crankset – a crank with small mountain-orientated chainrings

compact drive system – the whole gear set up – cassette, derailleurs and cranks – for smaller mountain-orientated gears

cone spanners – flat spanners devised to access small spaces behind cones and lockrings

cones – conical shaped metals parts for the bearings to run in

crank bolts – bolts to hold cranks to bottom bracket axle

crank-removing tool – tool for removing cranks, strange though it may seem.

cranks – the two shafts that attach the pedals to the bottom bracket axle

crankset – the collective term for the left and right crank

crown race – the headset bearing surface that is attached to the fork, at the crown

crown race remover – tool for removing said crown race

crown race setting tool – tool for installing crown race

cup-and-cone hubs – hubs that have loose ball bearings and can be adjusted

cup-and-cone systems – hubs that have loose ball bearings and can be adjusted

derailleur – device that moves the chain over sprockets (rear derailleur) or chainrings (front derailleur)

diamond pattern – the standard term for the classic frame design

dishing stick – tools used for checking alignment (dish) of the rear wheel

drive train – pertaining to the drive (gears, chain, sprockets, pedals)

drive-side cone – cone on the gear/drive side of the bike or wheel

drive-side crank – or right hand crank

drive-side spacer – spacer on the gear/drive side of the bike or wheel

dropouts – the part of the frame that anchors the rear wheel

dual-pivot brakes – contemporary design brakes with increased power through dual pivot design

ergopower brake – Campagnolo's term for integrated brake and gear levers

eyeletted rims – rims with stainless steel inserts at the spoke holes

facing tool – a tool for flattening a surface of a tube (Head tube, crown race or bottom bracket)

fork crown facing kit – tool for squaring up fork crown

fork crown race – see crown race

fork ends – where the wheel is held in the fork (can also be called drop outs)

fork steerer – the tube that attaches to forks to the head tube

fork-end protector – small plastic part used for packaging bikes

frame alignment tool – tool for checking frame alignment (straightness?)

front hub – central element to the front wheel housing bearings and wheel axle

front-facing dropout – a rear dropout that faces forward, so the wheel is removed towards the frame

gear hanger – part of the frame that is threaded for the rear derailleur

gear ramps – elements pressed into the gear sprockets to enhance and assist gear shifts

gear shifters – levers that change gear

granny ring – on a triple crankset it is the smallest chainwheel

head angle – angle of the head tube

head tube – frame tube that holds the forks

head tube reamer – tool that prepares the head tube for the headset fitting

headset or Aheadset – the bearing parts for the forks

headset cup remover – tubular steel tool that splits and allows the headset cups to be 'knocked-out'

headset cups – the parts that hold the bearings for the steering

headset press – tool used to push-fit headset parts (cups)

hub – the part of the wheel that holds the axle and the bearings

hub body – the main part of the hub, also known as hub body

ISIS – international standard type bottom bracket design

jig – a device for holding something while working (frame jig, wheel jig, etc.)

jockey wheels – small wheels inside the rear derailleur

lacing – pattern of the spokes in the wheels

lever hoods – rubber covers that protect the hands from the brake levers

lock nut – nut that is tightened onto another part to prevent it from moving

lock rings – as above (usually bigger)

long-cage mech – rear derailleur with a long cage for wide ratio gears

mech – another word for derailleur

octalink cranks – a Shimano pattern design for fixing cranks to axle.

over-shifts – where the gear mechanism travels too far with one gear shift

parallelogram machanism – derailleurs have a parallelogram design with plates that move about pivots to change gear

Park Tools – USA quality tool brand

pawls – small metal parts that engage inside the freewheel mechanism and make the clicking ratchet sound

pedal cleats – plastic plates that engage with the pedals to keep the rider fixed in to the bike

pedal threads – the threads that affix the pedals to the cranks

pitting – damage to bearing surfaces

play – when the bearings come loose this is referred to as 'play'

podger – a tool for poking holes

presta – high pressure valve for racing bike inner tubes

QR skewers – the central shaft on quick release lever systems, usually refers to the complete mechanism

quill stems – a stem design from before Aheadset systems, uses a quill that is tightened into the head tube

ratchet ring – the inside part that creates the freewheel

rear dropout alignment tools – tool used to check and repair rear dropouts

rear dropouts – where the wheel is inserted and held in the frame

rear mech – or rear derailleur

record hub – top of the range hub by Campagnolo

removing cassettes – see cassettes

rim eyelet – a steel insert into the (usually) aluminium rim that holds the spoke nipple

rim hole – the hole at which the spoke is attached to the rim

saddle-to-bar drop – the distance between the top of the saddle and the centre of the handlebars

schraeder – a valve design, similar to those used on car and motorbike tyres

seat tube – the tube of the frame that the seat post fits into

seat tube reamer – a tool used to clean out the seat tube

self-centring jaws – jaws that adjust and move together independently

Shimano STI lever housings – the body that holds the gear and brake shifting assemblies

sidewall – the side of a tyre (not the tread)

skewer – see quick release skewer

soft drift – a tool that can be used to hammer sensitive parts without damage

spacers – used at the Aheadset to adjust the height of the handlebar stem

speedplay cleats – specific cleats used for speedplay pedals

spoke keys – tool devised to fit spoke nipples

SRAM Red – a pro level groupset made by SRAM

SRAM/TRUATIVE cranks – a brand name of cranks made by SRAM

star nut – small threaded widget that attaches the Aheadset top cap to the fork steerer

star nut-setting tool – tool for inserting the star nut into the fork steerer

stays – the chain or seat stays or mudguard stays

steerer cutting guide – a clamp with a slot in it for sawing the fork steerer

stem – usually refers to the handlebar stem extension that attaches the handlebars to the fork steerer

top tube – the tube that connects the seat tube to the head tube

triple drivetrain – three-ringed cranks

truing – straightening (wheels)

tubulars – tyres that have integral inner tubes stitched into them

tyre boots – larger puncture patches that can repair ripped tyres

unship – fall off (re: chains)

vernier calipers – engineers tool for measuring

wheel dish – the shape of the wheel

wheel dishing stick – see dishing stick

wheel jig – or truing stand, used to true and adjust wheels

wheelbase – distance between front and rear wheel axles

INDEX